Although my name appears on the cover, the entire contents were inspired by the Holy Spirit. If anything is accomplished through the publishing of this book, it will be because of God's doings and not mine; and He, not I, must get the credit. God inspired it; I merely recorded it.

Brother Don

Let Your Light Shine

99 Easy Ways to Witness

by Brother Don

Published by:
Empire Publishing, Inc.
Box 717
Madison NC 27025-0717
336-427-5850

—publishers since 1974—

ISBN Number 0-944019-25-0
Library of Congress Catalog Card Number 98-070873

Additional copies of *Let Your Light Shine* are available from your local bookstore or from the publisher. Volume prices available for volume buyers.

Empire Publishing, Inc.
PO Box 717
Madison, NC 27025-0717
Phone: 336-427-5850
Email: movietv@pop.vnet.net

Manufactured in the United States of America

Cover Design by Orrin Lundgren and Rhonda Lemons

Scripture on cover is from Matthew 5:16 in the *New Revised Standard Bible*.

TABLE OF CONTENTS

Acknowledgments

Like most books, this one was easier to compile because of many wonderful people. To all who contributed their time, talents, and efforts, I am deeply indebted.

My journey down life's road has been a pleasant experience, and friends have been numerous. For me to mention everyone who has been a part of seeing this book become a reality, would be a difficult task because there were so many. To those whose names do not appear, I apologize, as you were not deleted on purpose.

I want to especially thank the following people who have influenced me in some way:

I thank God for placing Noreen in my pathway forty years ago. She has been a faithful wife and pal and has always allowed her spiritual light to shine so others may see Jesus in her life.

I have fond memories of my mother who first introduced me to the Bible and its rewards.

My two daughters, Rhonda and Doneen, have lived their entire lives in such a manner that has been pleasing to their mother and me. It is our belief that their lives have been pleasing to God as well. Rhonda was the overseeing editor of this project, and her supervision was a necessity in bringing the book to completion. Doneen assisted her when she was needed.

My in-laws, Bertha and Ervin Cox, have lived lives that have been a constant reminder that Jesus has been their guiding light down the trail of life.

I thank my grandson, Nathan, for bringing joy into our lives and for allowing us to be an important part of his life.

I appreciate my son-in-law, Stephen, for his straightforward views about his faith in God.

To Debra DeLancey, I owe a debt of gratitude for putting forth the extra effort that was required to produce this project. Her expert knowledge in production work was a tremendous asset that proved to be invaluable.

Appreciation goes to Orrin Lundgren for his talents in drawing the majority of the illustrations. His cartoon drawings brought amusing action to some serious topics.

To Ashley Holt, I owe thanks for the many hours she spent proofreading every page of the manuscript. Her efforts allowed the project to move along at a faster pace.

To Reverend Steve Joyce, I am deeply indebted for his encouragement, suggestions and overall excitement about this book and for answering the call to write the afterword.

To my friend, Carl Adkins, who, through the years, has always addressed me as "Brother Don."

A special thank you goes to the following ministers: Bill Lovings, Ron Williams, Bob Burnett, Jerry Waugh, Mike Collins, Evelyn Browning, Pat Robertson, Lee Ellis, Bob Harrington, Robert Bogan, and Billy Graham.

Also, to all those who are mentioned within the text, I thank you for being part of my spiritual life and for becoming a part of this book. Thank you! Thank you! Thank you!

Buddy Ames
Kerry Andrews
Tim Ashburn
Mike Boulding
Jeff Bowen
Anita Bryant
Burgess Trucking Company
Bill Bright
Jimmy Carter
Rosalyn Carter
Jack Chick
Viggo Christianson
Jerry Clower
Comer Photography
Bill Cosby
Donna Douglas
Elwood Evans
Lynn Flowers
Steve Flowers
Evelyn Foulks
Bill and Gloria Gaither
Greg Gentry
Marvin Hensley
Kathy Hildreth
Tommy Hildreth

Connie Hopper
Doug Jones
Bil Keane
Doyle Lawson
Billy Mills
Jim Moss
John Moss
Irene Nelson
Donald W. Patterson
J. P. Patterson
Sherman Pippin
Jim Prince Family
Brenda Roberts
Jean Roberts
Darrell W. Robinson
Kathryn Self
Ricky Skaggs
Peggy Spaugh
LeRoy Taylor
Verna Thomas
Warren Trucking Company
Ronnie Webster
Sharon White
Flip Wilson
Chubby Wise

Again, I am truly grateful for everyone's encouragement and untiring support.

**Dedicated
to
our Lord and Savior,
and to everyone who has the desire to become a
better witness for Jesus Christ.**

ATTENTION, READER

IMPORTANT! *Please read the introduction first!*
It is well known in the book trade that most introductions are skipped over and not read so that the reader may get right into the first chapter. I urge you not to bypass the introductory pages, as they explain how and why this book became a published work. It is very important that you know why this book was written prior to reading the chapters.

Other items for your information:

•Scripture quotations noted "KJV" are from the *King James Version* of the Bible.

•Scripture quotations noted "NRS" are from the *New Revised Standard Version* of the Bible copyright © 1989 by the Division of Christian Education of the National Council of Churches of Christ in the United States of America. Used by permission.

•Scripture quotations noted "TLB" are taken from *The Living Bible* copyright © 1971 by Tyndale House Publishers, Inc. All rights reserved.

•Scripture quotations noted "NIV" are from the *Holy Bible, New International Version* copyright © 1973, 1978, 1984, by International Bible Society. Used by permission of Zondervan Bible Publishers. All rights reserved.

•Scripture quotations noted NEB are from the *New English Bible, The New Testament* © 1971 by he Delegates of the Oxford University Press and the Syndics of the Cambridge University Press.

•The "✝" symbols throughout the book indicate some of the special ways to witness that the author wished to bring to the reader's attention.

•Unfortunately, there is not a word in the English language that is equivalent to "he or she." Therefore, for the sake of simplicity, the publisher has sometimes elected to use the word "he" when referring to a single person of either gender.

Rhonda K. Lemons
Editor

Introduction

How and Why this Book Was Written

The concept of having this book written and published came into being in the year 1993. That was the year Pastor Lee Ellis was invited to conduct a three-night revival at our church. One evening after that night's revival service, Reverend Ellis put a little extra spark into his message by giving everyone in attendance a small aluminum cross as he was saying his good-byes at the front door of the church. As the cross was placed into my hand, I promptly dropped it in my pocket without much thought at that time about the giving of the cross. Later that evening just prior to retiring, I retrieved the cross from my pocket for closer examination of what had been given to me. The cross was firmly attached to a four-page printed card, neatly folded, and small enough to fit nicely into a shirt pocket. On the outside of the card was printed, in large bold type, the words: **THE CROSS IN MY POCKET**, and on the back side was printed what Jesus said:

If anyone wants to be a follower of mine, let him deny himself and take up his cross and follow me. For anyone who will keep his life for himself shall lose it; and anyone who loses his life for me shall find it again. (Matthew 16:24-25 KJV)

As I opened the card that had the cross attached, I discovered a seven-verse poem written by Verna Thomas that explained what "The Cross In My Pocket Ministries" is all about. With the permission of Marvin Hensley and "The Cross In My Pocket Ministries" the poem is being reprinted on the following page.

THE CROSS IN MY POCKET
by
Verna Thomas

I carry a Cross in my pocket
A simple reminder to me
Of the fact that I am a Christian
No matter where I may be

This little Cross is not magic
Nor is it a good luck charm
It isn't meant to protect me
From every physical harm

It's not for identification
For all the world to see
It simply is an understanding
Between my Savior and me

When I put my hand in my pocket
To bring out a coin or key
The Cross is there to remind me
Of the price He paid for me

It reminds me too, to be thankful
For my blessings day by day
And to strive to serve Him better
In all that I do and say

It's also a daily reminder
Of the peace and comfort I share
With all who know my Master
And give themselves to His care

So, I carry a Cross in my pocket
Reminding me, no one but me,
That Jesus Christ is Lord of my life
If only I'll let Him be.

After reading the poem I quickly exclaimed to myself "I can do that!," and from that day until the present I have always carried the little cross in my pocket. I knew then that as a child of God I was weak in sharing the faith with others. I still am weak today in sharing God's word, but I am growing in the faith day by day, striving to do as God would have me to do. My conviction was strong but my witness was weak; however, since God calls the weak and the unqualified people to do His work I needed something to happen in my life to jolt me a bit so that I could become a stronger witness and a better Christian.

The "Cross In My Pocket" ministry was a giant turning point in my life. I became so engrossed in the cross witness program that I now buy as many as 500 crosses in one order. That was an easy way for me to begin my witness. Although, I did not know it then, that was the point in my life when this book actually began.

I, as most Christians, want to relate to others God's blessings and see them accept Jesus as their personal Savior; but how can that be done? What avenues may we take to obtain that goal? I believe most of us are not strong enough in the faith to start conversations with strangers, store clerks, taxi drivers, co-workers, relatives and others, talking with them about their salvation. Being quite honest, I am still weak in this area and I know there are thousands just like me. How about you, dear reader? Are you able to walk up to strangers and ask them, "Are you a Christian? Is Jesus Christ the Savior of your life?"

After dabbling a bit in giving crosses to others I soon began pondering over my thoughts that there *must* be other easy ways to witness our faith. The ideas began to come to me, and I started writing them down just for fun! The list began to grow, and one day I ran a count, and discovered I had scribbled down a dozen or so easy witness ways. I became quite intrigued with this simple way to praise God, so I kept writing them down. The next turning point came when

I stayed up a long while past my normal bedtime. The year was 1993. Then, it happened! I never heard a loud roar of thunder, nor did the earth shake, and I never heard the audible voice of the Holy Spirit, but I was convinced that God was conversing with me very clearly and the message was for me to continue gathering my thoughts and to put them in book form. Even the subtitle, *99 Easy Ways To Witness,* was established that early morning. At first, it was bothersome and mind boggling to even imagine that I was being called to oversee this project, being aware of my limited Bible knowledge; but within the same week I did indeed begin gathering more of my thoughts and ideas and was on my way answering God's calling. I knew that I was *not qualified* to compile a book on religion, especially on such an important part of Christianity as advising others about witnessing for Jesus. Then I wondered, "Are there not hundreds, maybe thousands, of books that have been written on witnessing already by qualified writers? Don't I need to study the Bible more before I tackle writing any book on Christianity? Who will will buy and read the book or will even take it as a free gift?" So many questions and so many doubts arose that I tossed my notes aside, and there they lay for almost a year untouched.

While attending a western film fan gathering, I became engaged in conversation with Bill Lovings. I casually mentioned to Bill that I had strong feelings that God was calling me to compile a book on witnessing. Bill is an ordained minister, and after I explained the concept of the book he encouraged me to, "Go for it; I think you should do it." I replied, "I will give it some more thought." Reverend Bill informed me that he knew of a couple of books on witnessing that might assist me in preparing for this book. He quickly went to his church supply house and mailed them to me. After reading the two soul-winning books, I was in agreement that both of those were dynamite publications. However, I was even more convinced that a book on easy witnessing may have a useful purpose for myself and others like me. Over the next three years I continued to gather easy witness ways, still not giving serious consideration about bringing it into book form.

At the beginning of last year I came to the decision that I was in a now or never situation. One nagging negative thought continued to bog me down. I kept saying to myself and others, "I am not qualified!, I am not qualified!" Somewhere along the way I was informed that in reality many of the unqualified are called by the Holy Spirit to do His work.

I Am Not Qualified

Moses had a speech impediment and did not want to obey God when he was called to lead the Israelite people out of Egypt and out of bondage from the powerful King Pharoah. Moses was saying to God, "Lord, I am *not qualified*; get a person that can do what you want."

And who did God call on to rid the land of that menacing giant Goliath? He called on whom most would consider to be the least qualified person in the land—David, a mere youth. Young David did not have armor, nor did he have a sword. He was armed only with a crudely made sling, a youngster's toy of sort, yet it could be deadly if used properly. His frail young body must have been a funny sight standing on the battlefield facing that giant warrior. David's brothers, among others, thought he wasn't qualified to go up against Goliath. We all know the end of that story. No, young David was not qualified, but God called him, and he answered God's calling.

When Jesus called the twelve men He wanted for His disciples, He chose those men that were not qualified. He chose people with various backgrounds: fishermen, tax collectors, and others. They certainly were not qualified, but they were called to do God's work just the same.

And then, there is the case of Gideon: When God

asked him to save Israel from the hands of the country, Midian, Gideon exclaimed, "But Lord, how can I rescue Israel? My clan is the weakest in the whole tribe and I am so weak and the least important member of my family." Gideon was telling God that he certainly was *not qualified*, but God answered him by saying, "I will help you and we will strike down all the Midianites together." Gideon was *not qualified* to carry out God's request, but nevertheless God called him.

Throughout time much has been recorded in the Bible bearing out the fact that many unqualified people have been called to perform certain feats and jobs that by reasonable standards would not be possible; but with God anything and everything is possible. I was able to tell myself that if I did undertake this project it would be written from the thoughts of a simple man. Perhaps this could be an advantage; only God really knows, and time will tell.

In preparation for this book, I have learned that I can be a witness to others. It was my desire to make the words, and contents of this book so understandable that a third grader would be able to read and comprehend it. No, I am not a qualified writer, but I have given it my best effort.

No Easy Witness Books Were Found

When the book idea first passed my thought waves I suspected that there would be many books in print in bookstores on the subject of "easy ways to witness." On my first journey to a rather large Christian bookstore, to my surprise, no books were found on the subject. Over the years I have continued to search out easy witness books. I was also surprised to learn that I was not able to discover any books that I would refer to as being an *easy* witness publication. Then I wondered, could it be that I had been allowed to stumble onto something that no one before me had done? Perhaps these easy witness *methods* are so easy to perform that others have considered them too trivial and shelved the idea. I don't know the answer to that question, but I do know that in searching over a long period of time through Christian bookstores and others, including national bookstores; I've never seen a book, cassette tape, videotape, or any other format that compares to this concept.

99 Easy Ways To Witness???

There are actually more than *99 easy ways to witness* within the covers of this book. The subtitle *99 Easy Ways to Witness* was given to my spirit at the same moment in time that the book idea was conceived. I have wondered, as have some of my friends, just why 99 ways and not an even one hundred ways. Most of them have said something along the line of, "At 99 you are so close to 100, why not even up the numbers to read *100 Easy Ways To Witness?*" I simply have interpreted the number 99 to be of a special meaning and thought perhaps the reason would be revealed later on.

In Luke Chapter 15 Jesus told this parable, *Suppose one of you has a hundred sheep and loses one of them. Does he not leave the ninety-nine in the open country and go after the lost sheep until he finds it? And when he finds it, he joyfully puts it on his shoulders and goes home. Then he calls his friends and neighbors together and says, Rejoice with me; I have found my lost sheep. I tell you that in the same way there would be more rejoicing in heaven over one sinner who repents than over ninety-nine righteous persons who do not need to repent.* (Luke 15: 3-7, NIV).

After reading the above lines of scripture I am of the opinion that the subtitle *99 Easy Ways To Witness* was God inspired and should remain as a reminder that as followers of Christ we are to leave the ninety-nine and go after the one that is lost.

Therefore, to the glory of God, this book is now in print. Let us all keep our eyes and ears open for more easy ways to witness to others.

CHAPTER 1
The Banana Lady

The person known as the banana lady is a very humble being. She loves God and wants the world and its inhabitants to know that Jesus is the Lord and Master of her life. † Each week she goes to the nursing home armed with the words of salvation and bags of bananas. She visits staff and patients, and while there, gives each a banana. When they see this saintly woman coming down the halls the residents yell out, "Here comes the banana lady!"

When I interviewed the banana lady, she was, at first, very reluctant to discuss her witnessing efforts with me. This Christian woman related that she would rather not include her spiritual efforts in this book. She further stated that she did not want to be recognized for anything she has been doing. "What I do at the nursing home, I do for the patients and to please God." Her words of wisdom by not wanting credit to be given to her is verified by opening the Bible to the beginning of the sixth chapter of Matthew and reading the words spoken by Jesus: *Be careful not to do your "acts of righteousness" before men, to be seen by them. If you do, you will have no reward from your Father in heaven. So when you give to the needy, do not announce it with trumpets, as the hypocrites do in the synagogues and on the streets, to be honored by men. I tell you the truth, they have received their reward in full. But when you give to the needy, do not let your left hand know what your right hand is doing, so that your giving may be in secret. Then your Father, who sees what is done in secret, will reward you.* (Matthew 6:2-4 NIV)

I respected her request not to use her name; however, I explained that I thought her witness ministry was very inspiring, and I felt it was too dynamic to exclude from the book. I was so impressed with her work for the Lord that I decided to use it as the beginning chapter of the book. Hopefully, others who read the "banana lady's" witness will be as inspired as I was. How about it? Are there any more "banana ladies" out there who wish to share their time and their witness with others?

CHAPTER 2
Home, Sweet Home

When visitors are guests in your home, is there enough evidence within to cause them to suspect that yours is a Christian home? Take a walk through your house. Is there a picture of Jesus on your mantle, wall, or elsewhere? Is the Bible conveniently located for all to see? Are there things on your walls and within your walls that would confuse your guests about your religious conviction? Since God is the center of Christians' lives, it is my belief that our homes should reflect our beliefs. A statue here, a picture there, a Bible on the table, or anything you like that would give your earthly home a heavenly look and would be a witness to all those who visit your "home, sweet home." † If the wall hangings in your home do not include a picture of Christ, why not please God, and witness to others by having one hung there this week?

CHAPTER 3
Bible on Wheels

Now here is a very easy way for you to inform others that Christ is the center of your life. Take inventory of Bibles on your bookshelf. If you are like me, there are several that you never use. † Choose one that is surplus and place it on the dashboard of your vehicle. It will be there as a witness to the driver and passengers, as well as passers-by at shopping areas, parking lots, and anywhere else you happen to go. Also, with a Bible in your vehicle, the availability of its contents will always be near by when you have the opportunity to read it. Christ's teachings inform us that we are to be His witnesses. Try this easy way to witness, and pray that lives will be affected by your effort.

CHAPTER 4
Be Happy

God expects His people to be happy. *Yes, happy are those whose God is Jehovah* . (Psalm 144:15 TLB) What does happiness mean to you?

† Another easy way to witness is to be a happy Christian. Just be happy—lay some happiness on everyone!

The dictionary defines happiness as being marked by great pleasure; enjoying one's condition; joyous; and even blessed. I've heard many explanations as to what happiness is, but how can we become and remain happy people?

Since January 3, 1988, I have carried a card in my wallet that gives, what I believe is, the best definition of happiness I have ever heard. I keep it on my person all the time, so I may read it to remind me of its message. I urge you to take a little extra time to read it through. Perhaps you will be in agreement with me that its contents have the potential to remind us to stay happy. Here is the explanation of happiness that I especially like:

HAPPINESS

Happiness is not a matter of good fortune or worldly possessions. It's a MENTAL ATTITUDE. It comes from appreciating what we have instead of being miserable about what we don't have.

Happiness is so simple, yet so hard, for the human mind to understand.

You have just read one of many definitions of happiness. Now let's take a look at what the Bible has to say about being happy. One of the definitions of "happy" in *Webster's Dictionary* reveals "to be blessed."

In turn, when "blessed" is searched out, it says "to make happy." To illustrate my point, I am reprinting the words of Jesus from the fifth chapter of Matthew:

- *Blessed* [happy] *are the poor in spirit: for theirs is the kingdom of heaven.*
- *Blessed* [happy] *are they that mourn: for they shall be comforted.*
- *Blessed* [happy] *are the meek: for they shall inherit the earth.*
- *Blessed* [happy] *are they which do hunger and thirst after righteousness: for they shall be filled.*
- *Blessed* [happy] *are the merciful: for they shall obtain mercy.*
- *Blessed* [happy] *are the pure in heart: for they shall see God.*
- *Blessed* [happy] *are the peacemakers: for they shall be called the children of God.*
- *Blessed* [happy] *are they which are persecuted for righteousness' sake: for theirs is the kingdom of heaven.* (Matthew 5:3-10 KJV)

Everyone wants to be happy. If you believe as I do, learn the above definitions of happiness, and relate them to others. † We Christians have learned that the first step in being truly happy is to put our trust in the Lord. So be happy. It pleases God and those who are around you in your journey through life.

CHAPTER 5
T-Shirts Are Happening

Over the past couple of decades the world has been bombarded with millions of T-shirts purchased and worn by people of all ages. Even today they are very much in demand. There are also sweatshirts, jackets, and other printed clothing items that have become the "in thing" to wear. They are available almost everywhere: beach shops, shopping malls, music shows, flea markets, and even Christian bookstores.

† I personally do not know of a more powerful, easy way to witness than to see a fellow Christian walking through a crowd with a T-Shirt, or clothing item, that relates a big printed message, proclaiming the gospel of Jesus Christ. There it is right in front of you. Will you read the message? Just try not to read it! I suppose that I have personally seen a thousand or more different religious/spiritual message T-shirts and related printed items over the years.

For the purpose of exploring this media of easy witnessing, I have compiled a list of a few printed shirts for us to be aware of their value in our Christian witness. How many of these have you seen?

- *I put all of my eggs in one basket, then I gave the basket to God.*

- *Jesus loves me this much (humorous).*

- *When God made me He was just showing off (humorous).*

- *Jesus loves you whether you like it or not (humorous).*

• *Directions to heaven: Turn right; keep straight.*

• *God's retirement plan is out of this world. Go for it!*

• *Jesus' All Star Team*
  * *Matthew*
  * *Mark*
  * *Luke*
  * *John*
  * *Peter*
  * *and Me*

• *What you are is God's gift to you.*
  What you do with yourself is your gift to God.

• *When all your hopes are shattered, when people disappoint you, remember there is someone who will never disappoint you — someone who will love you to the very end, and that someone is Jesus.*

• *If you are headed in the wrong direction God allows u-turns.*

• *As life got tougher, my faith got stronger.*

• *If you meet me and forget who I am, you have lost nothing, but if you meet Jesus and forget Him you have lost everything.*

• *Jesus is Lord of my life.*

• *Wise men still seek Him. Are you wise?*

• *Jesus carried a cross on His back for me. I'm carrying His name on my back for Him.*

• *7 Days without prayer makes one weak.*

• *Exercise your faith; walk with the Lord.*

• *In the event of rapture, you can have this shirt.*

• *Hang out with Jesus—He hung out for you.*

Because you are reading this book, it is my assurance that you have the desire to be a messenger for Christ. These shirts are available almost everywhere you may travel. The cost is low, and the rewards you receive will be very high.

† Peggy Spaugh related the story about how she witnesses every day at her workplace where hundreds of customers are exposed to the many religious T-shirts she wears. Peggy is an out-front cook and server at Herbie's Restaurant in Greensboro, North Carolina. Her employer leaves it up to the individual employee to wear whatever type of garment he/she chooses. Peggy chooses to wear T-shirts with a Godly message.

One day recently she was given a pretty shirt that did not have a spiritual message printed on it, and she wore it to her cooking employment. Regular patrons made comments about missing the shirts she usually wore. One gentleman customer related, "I have read a Bible message every day this week, and today it was missing." She assured him the message shirt would be back on the scene the next day, and, to this day, she continues this witness to the restaurant diners.

Now listen to this! Here is a real kicker—an idea I never would have dreamed up in a hundred years. When Peggy cooks, her back is toward the diners. † After being asked so many times to turn around so that customers could read the message that is printed on the front of her shirt, she decided to wear the shirt backwards. How about that! Now folks see the message on her shirt all the time while enjoying the meal that Peggy has prepared.

How about you? Are you ready to get involved in

what may be one of the easiest forms of witnessing? If you are ready, spend a few bucks for some shirts, wear them to malls, sporting events, school, and become a walking witness for all to see.

CHAPTER 6
Speak of the Devil

To those who may be wondering, Satan is alive and doing quite well throughout the world. He is going about doing his dastardly deeds that he hopes will keep people from knowing the truth about God's blessings for mankind. He is in the supermarkets where we shop. He is at our workplaces. He rides in our automobiles when we make our daily journeys in sometimes rush hour traffic to our place of employment. He is in our homes; and yes, as tough as it is to say, he is even in our churches. Recording artist, Ray Stevens, sums it up very well in a line from one of his comedy hit songs referring to Santa Claus, "He's everywhere, he's everywhere." That's where Satan is, dear reader; he is everywhere.

Don't picture him as he is depicted in movies, TV shows, books, jokes, and in general conversation. I do not believe the devil sports a red tail that protrudes to the ground. Neither do I believe he has horns coming through his skull. There is nothing in my Bible that indicates his appearance is like I just described. In fact, the Bible gives no description of Satan. I envision Satan being a beautiful creation with gorgeous, flowing, wavy hair, the body of a muscle-bound weight lifter, with face and eyes that would capture the attention of all who saw him. And as the human eye could see, he probably has an almost perfect and handsome specimen of a human body. Please keep in mind, this is my opinion of the way Satan may appear to mankind. Your thoughts on the appearance of the devil, in all probability, are different from mine. That's all right.

The reason for me believing the way I do is derived from several scriptures that tell me he is . . . *full of every sort of trickery and villainy, enemy of all that is good. . . .* (Acts 13:10 KJV) He certainly has his ways of deception that very well may include a desirable appearance.

Nowhere in the Bible have I been able to locate any reference to Satan's appearance, but it is my belief that he comes to us in many forms. 1 Peter 5:8-9 TLB warns us to *Be careful—watch out for attacks from Satan, your great enemy. He prowls around like a hungry, roaring lion, looking for some victim to tear apart. Stand firm when he attacks. Trust the Lord; and remember that other Christians all around the world are going through these sufferings too.*

All we need to do is: . . . *Resist the devil and he will flee from you.* (James 4:7 TLB) We are told that in the end, *the devil who had betrayed them will again be thrown into the Lake of Fire burning with sulfur where the Creature and False Prophet are, and they will be tormented day and night forever and ever.* (Revelation 20:10 TLB)

Flip Wilson became famous as the comedian who would blurt out, "The devil made me do it." For years audiences have laughed at references to Satan and his domain called Hell. But we Christians are aware that there is nothing funny about being in the clutches of the devil, being under his power, and spending eternity in a burning hell. I, for one, knew Satan's ways for the first forty-two years of my life. It is now very disturbing for me to relate this part of my life, but it must be told. Perhaps it will bring to someone's attention the mistakes I made by not accepting Christ for so many years and now realizing I am a victim of so many wasted years.

Although I really never gave it much thought at the time, I was a follower of Satan, and he had control of my life. As a born-again Christian, I can now see clearly that I was doing exactly as the prince of darkness wanted me to do. During that time I would have denied any alliance to anyone except God, but it would

have been a lie. I now know how people without Christ in their lives react because I have been there. Many who believe in God would never relate to having a relationship with Lucifer; but we Christians are aware that, according to God's word, we are either lost, or we are saved. If we are saved, we know where we stand. If we are lost, are we not a follower of Satan?

† So the next time someone says in conversation, "Well, speak of the devil," this will be your cue to witness by expelling, "I'll speak of the devil; I will tell you all I know about him and nothing is good." Hopefully, the Bible verses about him included in this chapter may be an aid for you to witness against Satan in your own way.

CHAPTER 7
Bumper Stickers

Bumper stickers have been used for several decades, and they are still quite popular with us Americans. We plaster them, not only on our automobiles, but on tailgates of trucks, farm tractors, sides of outbuildings, and telephone poles. You think of a spot, and probably a bumper sticker has found a permanent parking place. Almost every subject matter has been covered. Near election time there are more bumper stickers displayed than at any other time. Politicians know that bumper stickers are assets in getting their names before the voters. † Since political candidates rely heavily on bumper stickers, we Christians also could use this avenue as a way to get our message out to the people.

Here are a few examples of witness bumper stickers I have seen:

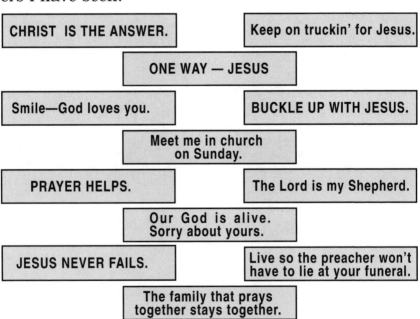

CHRIST IS THE ANSWER.

Keep on truckin' for Jesus.

ONE WAY — JESUS

Smile—God loves you.

BUCKLE UP WITH JESUS.

Meet me in church on Sunday.

PRAYER HELPS.

The Lord is my Shepherd.

Our God is alive. Sorry about yours.

JESUS NEVER FAILS.

Live so the preacher won't have to lie at your funeral.

The family that prays together stays together.

CHAPTER 8
Tell Others You Believe

Some Christians I have interviewed claim they do not have a testimony. Others have said they have one, but it is not interesting enough for anyone to want to hear. Still others have told me they have never given or been asked for their testimony. One person said, "I believe that someone who, prior to becoming a Christian, lived a somewhat-shaded and sinful lifestyle has a stronger, more interesting testimony to give than someone who accepted Christ at a very early age and has attempted to live according to God's commandments his entire life." This is a very humbling thought and my answer to that child of God is this: I believe that the strongest testimony would come from the lips of a person who has known Jesus as his personal Savior for almost an entire lifetime. Friends, to me, that is the greatest testimony that one could ever expect to hear, and it should be shared.

When you have in your possession the greatest news ever announced, why would one be so hesitant to share it with others? I believe that every Christian has a testimony. † I further believe that all testimonies should be shared. I know that some believers are not comfortable speaking of themselves as they fear others may see them as being boastful, but this is God's work. People all around you are hungry for the Good News, and we Christians believe that without Jesus they cannot have eternal life.

In my amateurish writing style, I will share a bit of my testimony. I would like to encourage you to sit down in a quiet setting with pen in hand and put on paper *your* testimony. You probably will be amazed at what will transpire from your mind to the paper.

My testimony is not of an earth-shattering nature.

I do not consider myself to have been a bad person, but I can relate that for the first forty-two years of my life, I was really convinced that I had complete control of my life and did not need guidance from the Holy Spirit. Oh, I believed in God and attended church with my family. I listened to Christian broadcasts on my drive to the workplace. I loved to attend Gospel music gatherings and did so whenever I had the opportunity.

Because I knew I was a lost soul, I was not able to talk about being a Christian. I could not enter into conversations about serving a living Savior. When people would begin questioning me about the experience of knowing God personally, I would break away and avoid questions about my salvation. I was very much aware that if I had died I would not have entered the kingdom of God. I knew that my soul was hell bound; as sad as this fact is to me now, I did not seem to care very much at that time.

In my mind, I had plans that sometime in the future, I would ask Jesus to come into my life; but not now, I would tell myself. I'm not ready! I knew what I should do, but I continued to live my life in a haphazard manner. Real, honest-to-goodness salvation was not important to me. When I attended worship services, I left whatever convictions I had in the church building to remain there until the next time I returned. I had thoughts of religious matters when I was away from church, but I was not the type of person to discuss them with anyone.

I now believe that real true Christian convictions begin when we leave the church property. That is when God puts us to the test. I now understand what is meant when Jesus said, *You are to go into all the world and tell the Good News to everyone.* God has called each of us to lift up the name of Jesus to everyone we come in contact with each day. If we do this, we please God. If we do not, we do not please God. God has shown me that I wasted many years living selfishly for my own interests.

As I mentioned earlier, I stumbled blindly through life until I was age forty-two before I made the commitment to serve the Lord and follow the ways of salvation. I have heard it said that the older a person becomes, the more difficult it is to make a spiritual change in his life. From my own personal experience, I believe this is true. Now I wonder: why do people shun God and wait so long before they accept His teachings?

One of the reasons that I waited so long to ask Jesus into my heart—the main reason—was that I did not feel worthy or good enough. Now I realize that I will never become worthy of God's blessings. The Bible states that all have sinned and come short of the glory of God, and this includes me.

Another reason, I believe, that kept me out of the fold so long was: I thought I would be giving up more than I would benefit from a conversion experience. Of course, that was foolish thinking. Satan had me in his clutches and was holding on to me, in hopes that I would ride along with him throughout this life.

As a Christian, I look forward to what God has in store for my life in the future. I now know that it is by grace I have been saved, through my faith. It is solely a *gift* from God and did not result from any works that I have done.

CHAPTER 9
Answering Machine

In these days of modern technology, God has allowed mankind to create things that make living here below a little more enjoyable. One of life's gadgets that I particularly enjoy is the telephone answering machine. It allows me, at my convenience, to return calls to those who have taken the time to phone. I can phone business acquaintances and friends; if they are not home, I can spout off for a minute or so telling the receiving party why I called.

Now you may be wondering, how can you witness with an answering machine? I am sure you will be able to devise your own way to witness, but Brenda Roberts does it this way: When her number is called, and no one is there to answer, the message reveals,

Thank you for phoning.... We're not here to receive your call; however, if you will leave your name and number we will gladly return your call. Please have a nice day and **may God bless you this day!**

✝ Using this simple technique, you may explore your mind for other messages that will witness via the answering machine—Bible verses, religious thoughts, etc. What could be easier?

CHAPTER 10
Roadside Signs

As we travel our highways and city streets, we are bombarded with signs from every direction. They are on business buildings, offices, traffic signs, and large billboards and advertise everything from beverages to automobiles. They are there for all to read, and boy, do we read them. Most travelers would agree that it is almost impossible not to read them. When a new sign appears on the scene it really stands out, and our natural curiosity commands us to read it.

✝ If we will take the time to search them out we can find many Christian witness messages on these roadside signs. You know the ones I am referring to. Some are crude, poorly-painted signs that are nailed to trees with messages as simple as "Jesus Saves" or "Trust in the Lord." Others may be professionally done on large billboards, reminding us to attend church or displaying a Bible scripture that proclaims the gospel of Jesus Christ such as: *Jesus is coming soon; God loves you; Work for the night is coming.*

One of my favorite sign sayings has been displayed on busy U.S. Highway 220 in front of the House of Stars in Madison, North Carolina, a business that retails storage buildings and carports. It simply reads, *John 3:16 says it all.*

Since I first began writing this book my eyes have been constantly searching the highways and byways for signs of religious themes. You never know where they will pop up, and you never know how they will read. Some are the quiet, subdued type of witness, such as the one I saw in California this past year. In fact, it was not a sign at all, but the message stood out very clearly. ✝ It was a huge, white cross up high on a hill, north of Hollywood on the Antelope Valley Freeway. The gigantic cross could be seen for miles.

On the other side of the United States, on U.S. Highway 220 just south of Greensboro, North Carolina, this stern message is attached to a tree: *Repent ... final warning.*

While driving on a two-lane road in southern Pennsylvania, my attention was quickly given to a large farm barn within only a few feet of the highway where a large sign had been painted on the end. It would measure approximately thirty feet wide by fifteen feet high in red and white letters. The message for all to see was: *At the end of the road you will meet God.* In smaller white letters on a blood-red background at the bottom of this marvelous witness sign was printed— *by area Mennonite churches.*

God's people are out there working. As I was driving into the city of Memphis, Tennessee, from the east on Interstate Highway 40 there was a gigantic (larger-than-most) billboard with the words, *I love you!* and was signed, *Jesus Christ.* What a sign! What a wit-

ness! Millions of travelers probably read that sign during that busy summer vacation time. Perhaps you, your church, or a local interest group could follow Memphis, Tennessee's Christian leadership and have a billboard welcome travelers through your town with your witness message.

On U.S. Highway 17 just a few miles south of Myrtle Beach, South Carolina there once stood a large roadside billboard that projected a message that read, *Without Jesus you will spend eternity with me.* At the lower corner of the sign, a picture of the devil was there to let you know that the message was coming from him. To illustrate the message further, a pitchfork was drawn on the sign. In our travels, we are seeing more and more religious theme billboards on the highways, which leads us to believe that more of God's people are making efforts to reach the non-believers and the unchurched.

Do not let Satan tell you it can't be done. With God all things are possible. Memphis Christians did it and so can you and/or your group. Look around and check out the possibilities. You may be the spark that will kindle a roadside sign project.

CHAPTER 11
Sing Those Sins Away

Do you attend Christian music concerts? My family and I attend several Christian music concerts yearly; we really enjoy getting into the spirit of worshipping by hearing God's word in song. Our favorite type of Christian music is Southern Gospel, and we enjoy hearing such groups as The Lewis Family, Cathedrals Quartet, Tony Gore & Majesty, Jeff & Sheri Easter, The Hoppers, Bill Gaither & Friends, The McKameys, and many others.

The singing Hopper family resides in our community. I have known Claude and Connie Hopper since high school days, and I have seen their ministry grow through the years. † They recently celebrated forty-one years of traveling the highways singing praises to our Lord.

Southern Gospel music has spread across our land and can be heard in practically all states with some regularity. It has grown to the point of being recognized as a very popular form of Christian music in our country. The music is upbeat, toe tapping, soul searching, and a dynamic witness for Christians and non-Christians alike. Southern Gospel music is very popular, and it continues to grow each year.

In the spring of 1997, in Greensboro, North Carolina, Bill Gaither and his Homecoming friends were hosts to more than 16,000 people who were longing for that Southern Gospel sound. The coliseum's advertising director, Kerry Andrews, announced that it was the second-largest crowd to attend a concert at the coliseum that year, winning out over secular acts including Reba McEntire, Kiss, and The Eagles. Andrews further stated, "I think this market is really strong for Christian concerts." (Gaither's 1998 Greensboro concert drew over 19,000.) According to Donald

W. Patterson, staff writer for the *Greensboro News & Record* newspaper, "Over the past four years, according to artists, promoters, and arena officials, Christian concerts in the Triad (Winston-Salem, Greensboro, and High Point, North Carolina, and the surrounding area) have grown to the point that they now compete favorably with secular acts." "That's a welcome change," says Jeff Bowen, booking/marketing director at Lawrence Joel Veterans Memorial Coliseum Complex in Winston-Salem, North Carolina, and a Christian music fan. "We used to do maybe one gospel concert a year that would do fair. Now we are doing anywhere from five to six that do well." Something is happening! Bill Gaither stated in a recent article, "I used to say that Christian music could never compete with country and pop music when it came to tape and compact disc sales, but in the last couple of years I have begun to wonder." At the Greensboro Coliseum it already is. Perhaps the trend will continue all across America and beyond.

What does God have to say about all this music stuff? Does He approve of it? Does He personally like music? In His word much is written about singing, dancing, and the playing of musical instruments.

Here are a few Bible scriptures I chose to illustrate the importance of music to God:

All these men were under the supervision of their fathers for the music of the temple of the Lord, with cymbals, lyres and harps, for the ministry at the house of God. Asaph, Jeduthun and Heman were under the supervision of the king. Along with their relatives—all of them trained and skilled in music for the Lord—they number two hundred eighty-eight . (1 Chronicles 25:6-7 NIV)

They send forth their children as a flock; their little ones dance about. They sing to the music of tambourine and harp; they make merry to the sound of the flute. (Job 21:11-12 NIV)

The book of Psalms has much to say about music including these Scriptures:

My heart is steadfast, O God, my heart is steadfast; I will sing and make music. (Psalm 57:7 NIV)

It is good to praise the Lord and make music to your name, O Most High, to proclaim your love in the morning and your faithfulness at night, to the music of the ten-stringed lyre and the melody of the harp. For you make me glad by your deeds, O Lord; I sing for joy at the works of your hands. (Psalm 92:1-4 NIV)

Have you ever attended a Christian music concert? If you have not, I strongly recommend that you make plans to attend one very soon.

There are many different styles of Christian music such as: Gospel, Southern Gospel, Contemporary Gospel, Church Choir singing, etc. ✝ You will be a witness to the Lord by being there, plus you will have all the fun reaping the benefit of a live Christian concert. ✝ To those who have attended, continue witnessing by going to future events, and *take others along with you!* Seek out those who, perhaps, have never attended a gospel music concert, and invite them to join you. ✝ You will be a witness to them, and hopefully, you will experience, as we have, your invited guests will be delighted with the afternoon or evening's concert and thank you for your invitation.

If you would like to be informed as to when and where Southern Gospel singers and musicians are going to be appearing in concert, there is a most informative publication available entitled *The Singing News*. My family subscribes to it and anxiously awaits its arrival each month. For subscription and/or sample copy information you may write Empire Publishing, Inc., Box 717, Madison, NC 27025-0717. Please include a self-addressed stamped envelope for a prompt reply.

CHAPTER 12
How's My Driving?

While driving a short distance to shopping areas or on longer weekend trips to a vacation spot, I usually do not travel very far until I am behind an 18-wheeler, a van, or other business-type vehicle that has a sign on the rear that reads something like this: *LIKE MY DRIVING? PHONE 1-800-I CARE.* This courtesy reminder informs motorists that if they have the desire, they may voice their opinion about the driver by telephoning someone who has authority regarding the business associated with the vehicle. That statement could be saying that the company officials involved want their trucks, vans, or other vehicles to operate on the highways in a courteous manner.

† Being courteous and considerate on the streets and highways is an excellent trait for Christians to have. Is this not another easy way to witness? Do we ever stop and think just how God expects us to conduct ourselves while behind the wheel of a motor vehicle? Does He expect us to adhere to the posted speed limit? How about deliberately changing lanes quickly in front of others? If our vehicle has unsafe equipment such as faulty tires, lights, etc., would He give us His blessings? We all know that God expects us to drive with a Christian attitude every day of every year; do we not?

On the other hand, how does He expect us to react if a motorist, without any consideration, pulls directly into your path and shows no sign of regret for his or her action? How about a quick slow down and jerky turn without any warning or any sign of a turn signal indicator being used? The humanistic reaction, perhaps, would be to raise our temperature to almost the boiling point, blow the horn loudly in rapid succession, and even shake our fists in disgust at the violator. It's my belief that God expects us to express our Christian faith and not allow other motorists to "get our goat," as the saying goes. Stay as calm as you can. Keep cool and run the motoring problems by a little test known as the Jesus test. It is a simple procedure. Just ask yourself, what would Jesus do if He were the driver of my vehicle and those things occurred?

I do not believe in long conversations when I can get right to the point. Therefore, here is the reason for the above: My friend Mike informed a group that he is able to follow Jesus' teachings about turning the other cheek when he has been wronged, lied to, talked about, and the like; but just let someone cut him off in a line of traffic and "WHAM"—he gets mad! He was in a kidding mode when he made that statement, but how many of us have a tendency to forget that we are Christians when we take the wheel of a motor vehicle? Is it okay to misbehave a bit, as if we left our Christianity at home or at the workplace? I know I have been guilty of this on occasion. I'm not yet perfect; I am still working on it. Perhaps, I would be a more courteous driver if I had the nerve to place a sign on the back of my station wagon that would contain my phone number for others to call me if I do not operate my vehicle in a Christian-like manner. The sign might read something like this: *Am I operating my vehicle in a Christian-like manner? If not phone 555-2222.*

There may be debatable conversations regarding this method of an easy way to witness. † However, it is my hope you will agree that as concerned motorists, we should operate our vehicles in such a manner that would please our Lord and Master and make Him proud of our driving habits!

CHAPTER 13
It's Puzzling to Me

Comedian Jerry Clower has much fun entertaining people by spinning his comical yarns about growing up and living around Yazoo City, Mississippi. † Mr. Clower is also known for telling others of his faith in the living God. A few years back he authored a book titled, *It's Fun Being Saved.* I, like Jerry, have also learned that it is fun being saved. Now, just for the fun of it, here is a puzzle based on the teachings of the Bible.

This rhyming puzzle may take you a few days to produce the answer, but hang in there; it should come to you after giving it considerable thought. When the answer does come, you are sure to say the clues were right on target, not misleading, nor was trickery used. So take your time. Read it through slowly and wait for the answer to come.

According to the story that was passed along to me, this puzzle was written by a lady in California in response to an offer from a gentleman in Philadelphia who would pay one thousand dollars to anyone who could write a puzzle he could not solve. The man failed to solve the puzzle and paid her the one thousand dollars. The answer is one word and appears in the Bible several times.

Of course the puzzle is here for you to have a little fun coming up with the answer and it will give you another avenue for witnessing. † Show it to your friends. Ask for their assistance in solving it. Another thought is you may want to relocate the puzzle by typesetting it on paper or stationery. † Make copies of it and pass them around. Isn't this a fun way to let your light shine for Jesus?

Adam, God made out of dust,
But thought it best to make me first.
So I was made before man
To answer God's most Holy plan.
A living being I became,
And Adam gave to me my name.
Thousands of miles I go each year,
But seldom on earth's soil do I appear.
For purpose wise which God did see
He put a living soul in me.
A soul from me God did claim
And took from me the soul again.
So when from me the soul had fled,
I was the same as when first made.
And without hands, or feet, or soul,
I travel on from pole to pole.
I'm very active day and night.
After my death I give great light.
No right or wrong can I conceive.
The scripture I cannot believe.
Although my name therein is found,
They are to me a garbled sound.
No feat of death troubles me;
Eternal happiness I'll never see.
To Heaven I shall never go,
Or even down to Hell below.
Now when these lines you slowly read,
Go search your Bible with all your speed.
For that my name is written there
I do honestly to you declare.

—*Author Unknown*

✝ Another idea would be to place a copy of the puzzle on the bulletin board or in the break room at your workplace with the following caption: *Do you know the answer to this puzzle? If you know the answer please contact (your name) in the (your department) as I really would like to know the answer.* ✝ When you are contacted about the puzzle the doors are opened wide, giving you the opportunity to talk to the person about spiritual things.

✝ If you know the answer to the puzzle, you could post the puzzle with another caption: *Do you know the answer to the following?* (Let's assume that the puzzle is posted on a Monday.) *Think on it all week, and I'll give you the answer on Friday if you are not able to solve it.* Most people are *not* able to come up with the right answer even if they ponder on it for a week. It is quite hard for most, but when the answer comes, folks say, "Oh, that's so simple; I should have known the answer."

✝ Another way to witness with this would be if you are a business owner or in a manager's position, you could create a contest for your office staff, sales group, or others. You may say to them that you want to create a little enthusiasm by allowing them the opportunity to come up with the answer to the puzzle. You may want to advise that everyone who comes up with the answer will receive from you (or your store or company) a steak dinner with all the trimmings at your local steak restaurant.

Here are only a few suggestions as to how this puzzle may be used to witness to others. Do you have suggestions as to other ways a Christian witness may be created using this puzzle? Why not write us your ideas? We would appreciate your interest, and perhaps, we would use your ideas in the next printing of this book.

You will have fun with this puzzler, and you may find that people enjoy being quizzed. Hopefully, you will get folks talking about the Bible who, perhaps, otherwise, would not.

My fellow constituents and I decided that for this puzzle to be a more effective witness, the answer to it would not be given within the pages of this book. It is our suggestion that you talk it up with others while searching for the answer. When getting others into the act you can honestly declare that you do not have the answer readily available, creating more interest for everyone. The answer, along with Bible references on the subject, will be promptly sent to you upon your request.

For the answer to the Bible puzzle send a SASE (self addressed stamped envelope) to: The Answer, Empire Publishing, Inc., Box 717, Madison, North Carolina 27025-0717 or phone 336-427-5850.

CHAPTER 14
Trucking for Jesus

While traveling America's highways I spend some of my driving time trying to keep my distance from the many tractor-trailer rigs. There seem to be more and more trucks on the road each year, delivering goods to their many destinations. In between trying to stay out of the truckers' way, I observe the signs, decals, and other items that appear on the trucks' exteriors. Over the years I have seen many things that proclaim the witness of Jesus Christ. I have observed the following printed messages for highway travelers to see:
- *Trucking for Jesus*
- *Jesus is Lord*
- *Glory to God on high*
- *God is my co-pilot*
- *And many others.*

† Burgess Trucking Company, which operates out of Charlotte, North Carolina, has *Safety is of the Lord,*

printed in large letters across the rear of their trailers for all to see. On the side of the trailer, there is another witness message that reads: *Jesus Christ is Lord.* Would there be any doubt in anyone's mind that the owners of Burgess Trucking, in addition to having trucking on their minds, also have the business of salvation on their minds?

Elwood Evans, a long-time truck-driving member of God's family, has proclaimed to me on a number of occasions how he witnessed while driving big rigs long distance. † Often he would go into a truck stop restaurant, and, as he would come in through the front door, he would yell out, "If anyone wants to talk about Jesus, come sit with me." This may not be an easy way for most of us to witness, but I think he has his own way of witnessing which should be included in this section about truckers. There are many drivers, as well as trucking companies, who have a strong witness for the Lord and are very comfortable in sharing it with others.

I know that I am barely scratching the surface on how truckers witness their salvation, but it is my purpose to keep this book as brief as possible and to the point. Hopefully, this episode will prompt truckers everywhere to write and relate ways they witness while going down the turnpikes.

If you are one of the thousands of drivers who pilot one of the eighteen wheelers up and down the roads, I urge you to take a while to ponder over how you can use your rig to witness. Just listen to God. He is talking. Are you listening?

† While driving on a Tennessee interstate highway, I saw, right on the back of a big rig's trailer, a sign that read, *Romans 8:31: If God be for us, who can be against us?* The trailer was one of 500 owned and operated by Warren Trucking Company, which is based in Martinsville, Virginia. Doug Jones, who is also an ordained minister, is the company's safety director. He informed me that they receive many telephone calls

and letters complimenting the witness stand they have taken. The witness sign that appears on Warren's tractor-trailers was conceived and carried out by its president, Buddy Ames, a Christian businessman who enjoys letting his light shine.

If you are an owner of a trucking enterprise, which comprises only a few rigs or a fleet of many, I encourage you to listen carefully. Is God telling you to follow in the footsteps of other truck owners who use their vehicles as turnpike billboards and witness to highway travelers coast to coast?

✝ If you are a wife, brother, sister, mother, father, or friend of a truck owner or driver, show him this chapter, and suggest ways he may witness with his truck.

Before ending this portion, there is another witness program pertaining to the trucking industry that warrants mentioning. There is a monthly publication that is published by an evangelical organization committed to winning truck drivers to Jesus Christ and teaching them to grow in their faith. *Highway News and Good News* is the name of the publication, and it is available free of any cost at selected truck stops and other locations. The truckers' publication is interesting, most informative, and spiritually uplifting. If you are not able to locate a copy you may consider writing the editor at their international office: *Highway News and Good News*, P.O. Box 303, Denver, PA 17517.

CHAPTER 15
Speaking of God!

✝ Speak of God in reverence. If we speak loosely of God, it will not be taken lightly by God. I know you will be in agreement when I say that a strong witness is to speak of God in ways that would honor His holy name and His kingdom. Have you spoken to someone today about God? Yesterday? This week? This month? You cannot keep yourself from hearing and seeing others speaking of God. The message is everywhere. It is printed on our United States currency and coins: "In God we trust." In the media we are constantly reminded that God loves us. We hear singers sing out, "God bless America," and "God bless the USA." Our Sunday school teacher relates to us about God's son, Jesus Christ, and how we all fall short of the glory of God.

All of us are on the receiving end of hearing others speak of God, but how many are transmitters, broadcasting God's name and His glory? That's what this chapter is all about. How can we make a turnaround? How can we gain knowledge to speak about God? One easy way is to buy yourself a simplified Bible concordance. The one I like is a Nelson's Comfort Print™ that has enlarged, easy-to-read print. Turn to the subject of God, and there you will find several hundred Bible verses with God named. Don't try to cover the entire subject contents; just choose some Scripture lines that are appealing to you and dive into the Word. You will quickly gather enough good material to begin your own central control headquarters to become a top-notch communicator for God.

Speaking of God in a positive manner is good; but speaking of God or about God in a vile, profane, or blasphemous way is not good. So we must be very careful not to speak of God or even mention His holy name in any way that would not be pleasing to Him. I often wonder exactly why so many of the film-makers, screenwriters, actors, and others in the movie industry constantly include scenes where the actors take the name of God in vain. In all probability, they believe that they are providing the movie and television viewers with exactly what most people want to hear and see. It is sad that so many people do not see anything wrong with using language that is degrading to the Holy Spirit. Yes, it is common today; however, the real question is not what you and I think about it, but what God thinks about it. Do you agree? One of the Ten Commandments which God gave to His people states very simply, but directly, *You shall not misuse the name of the Lord your God, for the Lord will not hold anyone guiltless who misuses His name.* (Exodus 20:7 NIV) When we demonstrate a disrespect towards Him, I believe it is a sign that God means little to us. When we use God's name to condemn others, we are showing hate instead of love, and that is a sin. We cannot love God and at the same time treat Him with disrespect. † Be God's witness by not using His holy name in a casual and improper way.

CHAPTER 16
Face the Mirror

Christians and non-Christians alike are constantly observing how others are dressed. I do not believe I will get any disagreements that, more than likely, women are more observant than men when it comes to clothing styles, color schemes, and the like.

Some of us are required to wear special uniforms in our work. Some places of employment expect a man to wear a coat and tie, but when we leave the job, most of us have the opportunity to dress in any fashion that pleases us. Some have their own thoughts as to how high to wear skirts, how tight (or loose) to wear jeans, pants, and other articles of clothing. Whether we like it or not, we are also judged as to the cleanliness of our bodies and dress attire.

Along the thoughts of dressing for worship, some believe that a suit and tie is the only acceptable dress for men, while others accept a more casual dress style. This observation is as far as I care to go on the subject, except I will reflect my thoughts that regardless what you wear to worship service, God looks on the inside, not the outside.

To sum up I believe there is a simple formula for Christians to use as a guide when their dress attire is chosen for the day. † When the dressing procedure is through, you simply face the mirror, take a close look and ask yourself, *Will my attire pass the Jesus test?*

CHAPTER 17
Changeable Signs

You may be asking yourself, what are changeable signs? They are rather large, oblong, billboard-type signs that usually are found in front of businesses. Most are approximately eight feet long by four feet high, sitting on four legs. Some have lights that burn so that night traffic may see the message that is displayed. The changeable sign has a plastic background with four tracks where flexible eight-inch black, plastic letters may be placed to spell out the desired message. You know these signs. They usually blast out to the drive-by traffic with such messages as *Bread 79¢ — Milk $1.59; Open all night; Lottery tickets sold here.*

I first became familiar with this form of witness when an article appeared in our daily newspaper around the year 1988. The article related how a convenience store had taken a stand to uphold the gospel of Jesus Christ by displaying religious statements of their faith such as, *If you are too busy to pray, you are too busy; If we let God guide, He will provide; Don't be caught dead without Jesus.*

At the time I thought, what a neat way to witness. Our own business is located beside busy, U.S. Highway 220, where it is reported that 20,000 plus vehicles per twenty-four-hour day pass by. We had a changeable letters sign already placed in front of our business location. I could use it the same way by placing spiritual messages on it and being a witness for Jesus. I thought, we can do that! We would be proclaiming the Gospel, and it would be so easy. I arrange the letters, and the sign sits there day by day giving motorists the Word twenty-four-hours each day. But what about some folks who may be offended by the messages displayed? Will we be known as religious fanatics? What about our family business? Will sales decrease due to our witness? Then I reminded myself that Jesus asked the question, "Are we here to please mankind or God?" Bingo! God won again. The same sign has been proclaiming God's glory since 1988, and during that time God has blessed my family so bountifully. Our business has progressed with higher sales as each year passes by. As far as possibly offending those who read our sign, we have instead experienced praises and appreciation for letting the traveling public, our customers, friends, and others know that ownership of the business consists of Christians who are willing to take a stand in His name.

So you may be thinking that you are not a business owner. How can you get into this type of witness? In comparison to other easy ways to witness contained in this book, a changeable letter sign requires a sizable investment. A new sign, offered at big wholesale-type stores, will sell in the range of two hundred dollars to two hundred seventy-five dollars. Each sign includes a full set of eight-inch plastic letters. † If the changeable sign ministry is of interest, you may want to consider placing your sign in front of a church, a vacant lot, or wherever space is available. You may want to set it in your front yard at your residence.

Some examples of sign messages are as follows:
* *See you in church Sunday.*
* *CH_ _CH What's missing? U. R.*
* *Life is fragile; handle with prayer.*
* *Expect a miracle.*
* *There is room at the cross for you.*
* *May God be with you.*
* *There is never a right way to do the wrong thing.*
* *The most important things in life are not things.*
* *Give Christ charge of your life.*
* *God will light up your life.*
* *Directions to heaven: Turn right; keep straight.*

- *Happiness is being saved.*
- *Christ is the answer.*
- *Smile; God loves you.*
- *Jesus never fails.*
- *At the end of the road, you will meet God.*
- *Sign is broken... Message is inside church.*
- *A Bible that is falling apart represents a life that isn't.*
- *Beat the Easter rush—come to church this Sunday.*

And in the humorous vein:
- *God doesn't believe in atheists.*
- *Notice: In case of nuclear war the ban on prayer in school will be lifted.*
- *Give your kids something to lean on — You.*
- *Everyone will live forever — The question is where?*
- *Work for the Lord — The retirement plan is out of this world.*
- *Be an organ donor — Give your heart to Jesus.*
- *Read the Bible — Prevent truth decay.*
- *As you hurry through your day — Take time to pray.*

With changeable signs that are placed beside busy highways and streets, it has been our experience that

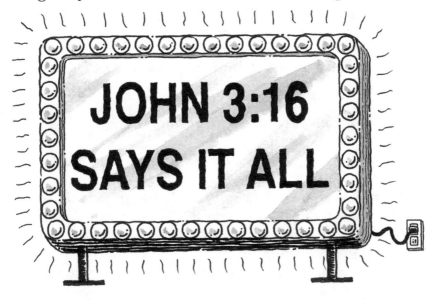

it can be read more easily if the message is limited to no more than ten words. Traveling past the sign at speeds of 50-60 MPH you are limited as to what can be read. Here is an excellent witness message, but obviously it contains too much copy and to the motorist it would not be read completely: *May the rest of your life, be the best of your life, and it can be if you place God first in your life.*

Again, based on our experience with this type of witness keep the message as brief as possible and right to the point.

If the changeable witness ministry is for you, you may find them at large stores such as Sam's Wholesale.

CHAPTER 18
Tell a Funny

You have heard it said, "Laugh and the world will laugh with you—cry and you will cry alone." The person who coined that phrase, in all probability, was a humorous individual; perhaps a good story teller of tales that were funny. It is true that people around the globe enjoy listening to stories that tickle their funny bones. The experts tell us there is something we all like to do that is good for us. It is laughter! Doctors say it works wonders in their patients' health. Pastors know that the most effective Christians always find something to laugh about.

† You can certainly witness to others if you choose your subject matter to include material based on Bible items and related things. As Christians we are judged every day in every way, including by the stories and jokes we tell. During my search for material for this book, I came across several joke books in Christian bookstores; but by far, the very best humorous religious book that I have seen was just published this past year. It's a dynamite book authored by Cal and Rose Samraand, and the title is *Holy Humor*.

The book is sprinkled with cartoons, amusing stories, quotes from famous spiritual leaders, one liners, bloopers, and the like. *Holy Humor* takes a light-hearted look at pastors, church life, marriage, politics, and the Christian life. It contains many cartoons by one of my favorite cartoonists, Bil Keane, whose nationally syndicated cartoon, *Family Circus*, appears in daily newspapers. † Bil often uses his cartoon to let his light shine by using religious themes for his *Family Circus* drawings. Trust me—this is a great book for pastors, lay persons, and anyone who in today's hectic world wants to take time to chuckle, giggle, have belly laughs, and learn that it is holy to be humorous! I have a copy of *Holy Humor* and would highly recommend that you get one too!

Do you tell jokes yourself? What kind of a witness do you present when you relate a humorous story to others? Of course, some jokes are funny to some and not so funny to others. When we take the stand to follow Christ, there are certain types of jokes that should not be voiced by us. For example, I find nothing funny about a crippled person who goes to a church to be healed, and when the so-called faith healer tells the cripple to throw away his crutches, he falls off the stage. Other handicapped-person jokes that some storytellers have thought funny contain references to people who stutter, alcoholics, overweight people, and the physically and mentally handicapped. I am aware that some comedians on television and other areas of entertainment earn a huge income by relating stories about the Polish, Jewish, people of color, and other races. However, it is my belief that relating racial stories, citing their different cultures and habits, is neither entertaining nor amusing. To further my thoughts, I believe as Christians there are stories we should neither tell *nor listen* to.

Let's suppose we are at the workplace, and a co-worker stops us saying, "Have you heard this one? There was this man who had two wooden legs, and he was burning leaves in his yard; his legs caught on fire, and burned up leaving him lying on the ground. They had to get a wheel barrow out of the tool shed to roll him back to the house." If you don't have a problem with a joke of this type you may give out a big Ha! Ha! Ha!, and go along your way. If you oppose to what I consider to be a crude, unfair, and unfunny ditty, here is the opportunity for you to spring into action. † With love in your heart for the storyteller you may want to not laugh at the story and gently say, "I know you wanted to get me into a jolly mood, but honestly, I would prefer not to hear stories that are unkind to persons who are less fortunate than most." † Or you may add something like, "I would not want to offend you, but as a Christian I find a joke of that type offensive," and explain to him in your own way why you feel as you do. If your faith is not strong enough and you don't have the will to say anything to the storyteller, that may inform you of the need to pray and ask God to give you strength for future confrontations of this type.

† Consider this situation: Let's say the story is being told to a group of people, and you may choose to do as others have done when the story gets to the point that you know the subject matter is of a degrading theme. You could quietly move out of ear range of the storyteller.

When Jesus related stories in parables, he often gave enough information for the listeners to begin searching out their own thoughts. That is what I am trying to do: give you my thoughts, present a few illustrations and let you, the reader, decide how you can handle the situation. Perhaps a decision can be reached by using what I simply call the Jesus test. Who is more the sinner, the teller of a distasteful story or the person who listens to the story and says or does nothing?

Some may question this issue by saying, "But I don't want to hurt my friend's feelings. I may offend him." At this point I will just say, the choice is yours! I'm only the author. I suggest that you do as you feel led.

When you tell humorous stories, choose your material carefully. Folks will still laugh and enjoy a story that is not filled with dirty words and uncomplimentary situations. Bill Cosby has proved that fact during his entire career as an entertainer and funny man who uses clean family humor. He has confronted fellow comedians and advised them to, † "Keep your act clean guys." It has truly paid off for him as he is one of the most successful comedians who has ever graced an audience.

Here are a few jokes along the line of easy ways to witness that you may consider telling:

The boy listened closely as the Sunday school teacher read the Bible. "May I ask a question?" he asked.

"Sure. Go ahead. Ask your question," replied the teacher.

"Well, the Bible says that the children of Israel crossed the Red Sea—the children of Israel built the temple—the children of Israel did this, and the children of Israel did that. Didn't the grown-ups ever do anything?"

*   *   *

"Who is the perfect man?" the preacher cried. "Is there such a man? If anybody has ever seen a perfect man, let him speak now!"

A small, nervous man stood up in the rear of the room. The preacher looked at him in astonishment.

"Do you mean to say, sir, that you know who is the perfect man?"

"Yes, sir."

"Who is he?"

"My wife's first husband."

*   *   *

The members of a Methodist women's church society became disturbed because a widowed church member and her three daughters were not coming to church services. After an investigation they learned that the reason was because the family didn't have suitable clothes for attending church. The women got together and bought a generous supply of clothing for the widow and her daughters. The next Sunday the widow was in church, but the girls were missing. The mother thanked the ladies for the clothes and explained, "The girls looked so nice that I sent them to the Presbyterian church."

*   *   *

"How late do you usually sleep on Sunday mornings?"

"It all depends."

"Depends on what?"

"How long the sermon lasts."

*   *   *

The hat was passed around one Sunday morning in a tight-fisted church. The hat was returned absolutely empty.

The pastor raised his eyes toward heaven and said reverently, "Oh, Lord, I thank thee that I got my hat back."

*   *   *

"Does your husband attend church regularly?"

"Oh, yes. He hasn't missed an Easter Sunday since we were married."

*   *   *

"Now there is even a dial-a-prayer for atheists."

"You call the number, but no one answers."

Go ahead, tell a funny, but make it pleasing to God when you do!

CHAPTER 19
Give a Book

Most folks are pleased to have someone take the time to give them a gift. † This easy witness suggestion is to give a Christian book to someone. There are many good titles available through Christian book stores, and you may choose one of your favorites to give.

If you are giving a book to a person who has been saved through the blood of Jesus and is living the Christian life, one of many hundreds of titles would probably be acceptable. But if you want to give a book to a person that is not within the fold of God, there is one book that I recommend over all the others I have seen. It was penned by Pat Robertson and entitled, *Answers to 200 of Life's Most Probing Questions.*

The unsaved have interesting and inquiring minds. They ask questions, and they demand answers. That is where the answer book comes into play. Chapter One begins with questions and answers that resulted from a "Gallop Poll" investigation where the pollsters went out into the streets to ask people, "If you could ask God just one question, what would it be?" Of all the thousands of people interviewed, I found it quite interesting to learn the top ten questions that resulted from the survey.

Here are the top ten questions that people asked:
1. *Why is there suffering in the world?*
2. *Will there ever be a cure for all diseases?*
3. *Why is there evil in the world?*
4. *Will there ever be lasting world peace?*
5. *Will man ever love his fellow man?*
6. *When will the world end?*
7. *What does the future hold for me and my family?*
8. *Is there life after death?*
9. *What is heaven like?*

10. How can I be a better person?

The author dives into other questions and answers that will be helpful for anyone who desires answers that get right to the point and are explained in simple everyday terms. Other subjects include these:
- *Will there be pets in Heaven?*
- *Should a Christian pay taxes?*
- *Are suicide victims forgiven?*
- *How can I know God is real?*
- *Where did all the races come from?*
- *Does the Bible teach evolution?*
- *What is sin?*
- *Does the Bible teach that once I am saved I am always saved?*
- *How powerful is Satan?*
- *What is the mark of the beast?*
- *What is hell like?*
- *If God is love, how can He send anyone to hell?*
- *What is the greatest sin?*

In addition to the book, *Answers to 200 of Life's Most Probing Questions*, I highly recommend the following books on the subject of witnessing: *Witnessing Without Fear* by Bill Bright—it goes into simplified detail about how to share your faith with confidence, and *People Sharing Jesus* by Darrell W. Robinson—this book gives a natural, sensitive approach to helping others know Christ. All three are published by Thomas Nelson Publishers, and are available at bookstores almost everywhere.

There are many books available in bookstores, but I favor *Answers To 200 Of Life's Most Probing Questions.* I use it often in an effort to learn answers that aid me in growing spiritually. Do you know of someone who is searching for answers and might benefit from this book? It could help that person grow in the spirit. Be a good witness; buy it, and give it to him or her. Again, if you are not able to find a copy, send a SASE to the publisher of this book for assistance in locating one.

CHAPTER 20
Keep Christ in Christmas

When the Thanksgiving holiday is behind us, and the year end is just before becoming a reality, there within lies the plateau of all holiday seasons—Christmas. With Christmas at hand the time comes to go to the attic and bring down Christmas decorations. Get out the Christmas tree that has been neatly stored in the same cardboard box that originally housed the tree since it was purchased at the variety store. How about that large Santa Claus face that lights up a darkened night and all the other Christmas items used to satisfy our urge to let others be aware that we are in the Christmas spirit? Hey, wait a minute, what are we celebrating anyway? Of course, everyone knows the real reason for celebrating Christmas—what would you think about changing your decorating theme this year by including items that depict the birth of Jesus Christ?

✝ Suppose you place a silk ribbon on that beautiful door wreath that reads "Silent Night, Holy Night?" ✝ A manger scene placed in your front yard all lit up by flood lights would tell others that Jesus is in your thoughts.

✝ You might even stake a sign in your yard that reads *Happy Birthday Jesus!* Sure, the neighbors may include you in their across-the-back-yard-fence chit-chat. You may even be accused of being one of those persons who take religion to the extreme—you know, like one of those religious fanatics. The flamboyant preacher/motivator, Bob Harrington, known as "the chaplain of Bourbon Street," said that "A religious fanatic is someone who is more in the spirit than you are."

As a part of your witness, keep Christ in Christmas as much as you can; your holiday season will surely be brighter and your household blessed throughout that special time of the year. God guarantees it.

CHAPTER 21
Fly a Christian Flag

I discovered this form of witnessing to others by way of flying a Christian flag about one year ago. With the family business being located on a busy U.S. Highway, we have always used flags of some type mounted on flagpoles for decoration and to attract attention to our establishment.

When the time came to order a new supply of flags, I saw Christian flags offered in the catalog. Routinely, I order state and American flags, but the idea came to me that displaying Christian flags would be another easy way to witness. When the flags came I quickly opened the package. One would have thought that I had never seen a Christian flag because when I unfolded one, I stared at it in amazement. The Christian flag is absolutely beautiful.

Then I wondered, since I had only seen a few Christian flags outside of a church, would the highway travelers be able to identify it? After all, it's red, white, and blue, like so many other flags. After hoisting it up on one flagpole where an American flag was, I went to the second pole and attached another one. This one was blowing in the breeze without another flag over it. There it was on a twenty-foot flagpole moving gracefully with the wind.

Just think, they are standing tall and witnessing to beat the band to anyone who cares to admire them. As I see them each day I am still amazed and puzzled as to how easy a witness this is. I now know that passersby do, indeed, know what kind of flag it is, as many have commented about it, and several folks have inquired as to where they may purchase one. I usually keep a few extras so I can quickly satisfy their desire to own a Christian flag. ✝ So, here is another easy way you may witness to others and yourself. Think about it! How can *you* use the Christian flag as a witness to your faith?

CHAPTER 22
Witness after Death

Have you ever thought about witnessing to others when your time comes to leave this world and enter into God's heavenly kingdom? I am aware that most folks do not want to discuss the possibility of death ever occurring. We know that it will happen, and we say we will talk about it *someday, but not now*! Many will say, "when it happens it happens, but I don't want to think about it now." Death is reality just as life is reality.

At the time of this writing I am sixty years of age, and hundreds of people I have known have passed on to their place in eternity—friends, school chums, my mother and father, neighbors, and church friends—so death to me is a real item of conversation. I personally have no problem with either talking about death or accepting it as a vital part of life. In fact, those who know me are aware that I am known to make statements in reference to bidding this world good-bye, such as my being ready to go to my heavenly home *today*! I have found that bold statements like this have a tendency to upset folks, but I am sincere. I am a Christian and saved by God's grace, and when my heavenly Father calls me home, I will be ready to go. I firmly believe that if Christians could rise above this world we now call home, take a peek over on the other side, and see everything that our God has prepared for those who love Him, we all would be ready to leave today—right now!

How can Christians witness to those left behind after we are gone? I like to use the word "transferred" rather than saying, "death." When our lives end on this earth, hopefully, we will leave a witness of our lives lived. I see several ways we can witness after our transfer from this world. ✝ First, the lives we have lived will bear witness to others—after death, we will be remembered for the seeds we have sown.

✝ Another after death witness would be to write your own newspaper obituary and have it on file with your pre-arranged funeral plans. I have already written mine, and it is on file with the funeral home where Noreen and I have already pre-arranged everything possible with the director. In addition to those items, we also have a burial site that has footstones already engraved with all pertinent information except our departure dates.

Now, do not think that I am a morbid person who delights in speaking of gloomy and gristly things. I am a realist; I know that at some point in time I will cross over, and my life on earth will be no more. Reverend Jerry Falwell said on one of his television broadcasts recently that "If I only had ten seconds to try to bring a lost person to Christ, I would simply say you have a choice. You can be born once and die twice, or you may be born twice and die only once." So therefore, I, along with others, will only die once."

Recently, I have begun to notice that obituaries revealing a person's religious convictions are appearing more and more in our daily and weekly newspapers. Church membership mentions in obituaries have been included for many years, but lately they have become more God loving and personal testimony-type obituaries. Here's what I mean. Noreen recently brought to my attention an obituary that impressed her, and after reading it, she cut it out of the newspaper and saved it. What a wonderful person the lady must have been. I wish that my family and I could have known her. To illustrate my point, and with permission of her family, the announcement of her departure is being reprinted on the following page.

Elsie Prince

On Wednesday, August 21, Elsie Prince chose to join her Savior, Jesus Christ, in Paradise. Her full-time job was a servant to her family, her community, and especially to her Lord.

Elsie was known as "Supermom," not only to her own children, but also to those in her church family and community. In lieu of flowers, all those who wish to continue Supermom's nursing of Jesus' children, can send contributions to Greensboro Youth for Christ, 824 S. Aycock Street, Greensboro, NC 27403, or Friendly Hills Presbyterian Church Building Fund, 201 College Road, Greensboro, NC 27410.

A gathering of friends will be held at Friendly Hills Presbyterian Church, 201 College Road, from 7-9 p.m. Friday, August 23.

Elsie had a sparkle of Jesus' love that showed in everything she did. Everyone desiring to celebrate that sparkle or seeking to have that sparkle, is invited to attend a celebration service at Westover Church, 505 Muirs Chapel Road, Saturday, August 24, at 2 p.m.

Until they see each other again in Paradise, Elsie leaves behind her husband, Jim Prince; five children, son Andy Prince and wife Kristine, daughter, Charlotte Smith and husband, Rodney, son, Matthew Prince, daughter, Katie Prince, son, Noel Frederick Prince; grandson, Caleb Smith; and stepmother, Alice Butler.

So there it is. Perhaps God has revealed to you through me a way to witness that you may never have thought of before. Now you know how to witness *after* the soul leaves the body.

CHAPTER 23
Hallelujah Taxi Service

If you have gotten through the book to this chapter and have not found an easy witness method that will work for you, perhaps this is the one that you will be comfortable with. I call it the "Hallelujah Taxi Service." This could be you. All you need is an automobile, a driver's license, and an hour or two of your time each week.

The next step in becoming a transporter is to phone, or better still, make a personal visit to your church office. You need to speak directly to the person who answers the church's telephone—the pastor, assistant pastor, the secretary, or other. † Advise that person you have decided that you want to better serve your church, and be a stronger witness of your faith by offering transportation for those persons who do not have transportation to and from worship services. You may, at this time, ask one or all of the staff if they have knowledge of persons who could use your services.

Let's examine a few folks that would benefit from a ride to church:

- *Of course, there is the elderly generation.*
- *Those who may not have a vehicle to drive to church.*
- *Persons without a valid driver's license.*
- *Those who due to an accident, surgery, etc. may not be able to drive themselves.*
- *Persons who won't drive after dark which eliminates them from attending night services.*
- *There may be parents who refuse to provide a church ride for their children.*
- *It is too far to walk, and it may not be safe to walk to church.*

Only a few circumstances have been mentioned here, and I am sure that if you want to get into this form of ministry you will discover dozens of reasons that your services will be needed. This is truly an easy way for you to witness. All it takes is an open heart to those who could use your "Hallelujah Taxi Service."

CHAPTER 24
Carry a Cross

I first discovered that I could carry a cross for Jesus at a revival service being conducted at my home church by a guest minister. He explained that the small aluminum cross, which measures about one inch, will fit inconspicuously into a pocket or purse. ✝ I carry the cross in my left pants pocket mixed in among my coins and pocket knife. I have been carrying it since that revival meeting night.

If you decide to form a habit of carrying the little cross, you will discover, as I have, that you will achieve many opportunities to witness to others in your day-to-day routine. Several times each day I reach for my pocket change—in restaurants, stores, etc., and out comes the cross with the pocket change. ✝ Sometimes the sight of the cross will begin a discussion such as, "Oh, I see you are carrying a cross; that's nice." A reply often will be, "Yes, I do. I'm carrying a cross for Jesus because he carried one for me." Jesus said, *If anyone wants to be a follower of mine, let him deny himself and take up his cross and follow me.* (Matthew 16:24 TLB) This is truly an easy way to witness to others.

✝ You may want to buy some crosses to give out to those in your church, your workplace, almost any place where you will come in contact with people from every walk of life. I'm sure you will discover, as I have, that the crosses are well received and appreciated. ✝ Business operators may want to place the pocket crosses in their businesses with a small sign, *Please take one with our compliments*, or *Carry a cross for Jesus*.

The Cross In My Pocket Ministry is a non-profit organization that is letting their light shine by providing small aluminum crosses, and encouraging Christians, even those who know a lot about the Bible, to share their faith in God. You can, in fact, let your witness count without saying a word. The cross is a universal symbol which speaks profoundly for itself. Sharing a cross with another person is a simple, effective, and joyful way to witness for Christ. Both lay persons and pastors have discovered countless ways to use these crosses in their ministry. The following are some ways that others have found helpful and are listed here for your consideration:

✝ Give the cross as a form of personal witnessing.
✝ Place the cross in the hand of a person awaiting surgery, facing a long illness, or residents of nursing homes.
✝ Tell the story of the cross to children. Distribute the cross at the close of a children's sermon or discussion session.
✝ Give the cross to high school and college graduates.
✝ Give to new members of the church.
✝ Send the crosses as Christmas cards, imprinted with your name.
✝ Utilize the pocket cross in a ministry to inmates of jails and prisons.
✝ As part of a quiet witness in the workplace, give a cross to colleagues and co-workers.
✝ Make the crosses part of a revival service.
✝ Sunday school teachers may give crosses to members of their class.

Verna Thomas composed a poem entitled *The Cross In My Pocket* that gives very meaningful explanations about this ministry. This powerful witness poem is printed in its entirety in the introduction of this book. The poem is printed on a card that comes with a cross attached and can be removed.

I strongly urge you to make the cross in your pocket

a part of your Christian witness. You will be glad you did! Jesus said, *Whoever does not carry his own cross and come after me cannot be my disciple.* (Luke 14:27 KJV)

The crosses are a very low-cost item and may be ordered from The Cross In My Pocket Ministry, P.O. Box 9711, Norfolk, Virginia 23505 or may be available at your local Christian bookstore.

WILL YOU CARRY A CROSS FOR JESUS?

CHAPTER 25
Coach a Team

If you have the knowledge and ability to lead a sports team of boys and girls in baseball, soccer, football, or basketball, you are given a wonderful opportunity to set a Christian example to those children. In your day-to-day contact with the team, you will be a guiding light to them, which will give you the opportunity to help mold their young lives in the direction they should go. † Being a Christian coach and using yourself as an example, you have the opportunity to inform the team members what is important in your life as well as what is not important.

I asked Steve and Lynn Flowers, husband and wife coaches, about their Christian witness while coaching youngsters in organized sports. "To be a subtle witness, we believe that it is necessary to present ourselves as a living example of what we would want our players to be. We project an image of love to them as a team and individually. With us, we don't put a priority on winning the game. We want to be assured that the children enjoy themselves and have a good time while playing. Winning the game is not the most important thing. When the teammates inform us they indeed had a good time playing we reply, 'Well, that's all that matters. We will be looking forward to leading you in another game very soon.'"

Steve further related, "Lynn and I are looked upon as being different when it comes to coaching teams. 'Win! Win! Win!' is not our chant. We never get hot under the collar, or rant and rave when a questionable call is made. We will calmly speak to the official, stating our belief on the call. After giving the official our views, we accept his decision for or against our team. For either of us to get angry, kick dirt, or raise

our voices, would destroy any Christian witness cred-
ibility that we may have. We stay calm and cool, as we
know those youngsters' eyes are on us and their ears
are listening."

Steve and Lynn said they love and guide the children as their own. They present themselves as different people both on and off the ball field. The image
they want to project to the team is that they are *in* the
world, not *of* the world.

When I asked them about how they might curb any
off-color language the young player may spout out,
Steve was quick to inform me that sometimes it is necessary to hold a five-minute Sunday School lesson in
center field.

By some people's thoughts and standards, many of
the words of disgust the players utter while playing
the games may not be in bad taste, but the Flowers
have a problem with some of the expressions that are
used by the youngsters. They are quick to correct
when, "Oh, God," "For Christ's Sake," "Oh, my God,"
"Jesus Christ," and words like these are used in disgust. As Christians, Lynn and Steve find those words,
when used improperly, are out of place and represent
blasphemy toward God.

Television programs and movies serve as conduc-
tors direct to the young minds, as the sitcoms and
films regularly use these terms, which may present
the image that it is okay to say them. But for players
or anyone to allow themselves to get hot under the
collar and spout out in anger, "Oh, for Christ sake,"
when a ball passes by them is not pleasing to God and
must not be allowed to go unnoticed.

Being active in sports is good for young minds.
There is much to be learned on the playing field, and
those who are Christian coaches have the responsibility of being Christian witnesses by seeing that the game
is played well and that good conduct is observed for
both players and coaches on and off the field.

CHAPTER 26
Put God to the Test

Give, and it will be given to you! Do you believe that statement? Jesus, during His life on earth, had much to say about giving, just as religious scholars today have much to say about giving. We obey God's message. We give our money to the church. We help feed the poor with our donations. We participate in worldwide missions funding.

What happens when we do not give our tithes and offerings to God's work? Does God take something away from us? What are the rewards of giving to God's work? Are there really rewards when we give?

I knew that before this book was finalized there must be something contained within on the subject of giving back to God a portion of what He has given to us. I am talking about the rewards of tithing—giving of our money and our time to God's work. It is a favorite subject of mine, as I want to please God. I have had it proven to me that when I give, more has been given to me. I have learned that God's shovel is larger than mine, allowing Him to shovel more to me than I shovel His way.

As Christians, we are aware that God's word commands us to give—and as His word proclaims—give freely. Many followers believe Him, but, for some reason or another, do not pledge or make allowances to give a percentage of their gain back to God's work. Some declare: "My employer does not pay me enough salary for me to give tithes and offerings;" "My spouse and I are on a limited income, so we certainly cannot give;" "I have too many bills to pay;" "The cost of living is too much today." The excuses go on and on.

Are you a tither? If you are not, you may become one today. Except for the improvements in your life, you will never notice the difference! When one agrees that the principle of tithing is right, it is remarkable how quickly problems and questions about tithing disappear when you do God's will. I have a strong belief that the real reason people refuse to tithe is because they have the mistaken idea that what we have is our own. We have a faulty conception of the Christian life. † Tell others you are a Christian, and you obey God by taking your tithe to the storehouse.

You may say, "I earn my money; why should I give it away?" I can understand how a non-believer could think that, but it is very difficult for me to comprehend how followers of Christ do not see the need to give tithes and offerings to God's work. Jesus had more to say about the right use of possessions than any other single subject. In fact, throughout the Bible there are 1565 references to giving.

Do not say you cannot afford to tithe until you have tried it. God will prove to you that you can afford to tithe. We must have the realization that our debt to God comes first. It is not just a good idea—God commands it.

I believe here would be a good place for me to insert a story, a parable of sort, that may illustrate to you, the reader, another side of tithing. Although we may find the story amusing, I believe it drives home a startling message about tithing.

"I want to tithe," a man told his pastor.

"I want to give 10 percent of my income to my church. When my income was $50 a week, I gave $5 to the church every Sunday.

"When I was successful in business and my weekly income rose to $500, I gave $50 to my church every Sunday.

"But now my income has gone to $5,000 a week, and I just can't bring myself to give $500 to the church every week.

The pastor said, "Why don't we pray over this?"

The pastor began to pray, "Dear God, please make this man's weekly income be $500 again so that he can tithe . . ."

I know that nothing new is being written here about giving that you have not heard and read many times before, but consider this: The Bible does not say give if you are out of debt; nor does it say to give your tithes if the cost of living is not too high. Nothing is mentioned concerning *not* giving if you are on a fixed income. I have not seen anything in God's word relating to any reason for *not* giving your tithe. It does say to, . . . *honor the Lord with the first fruits of all your produce; then your barns will be filled.* (Proverbs 3: 9 RSV) And the Scriptures also say, *Bring the whole tithe into the storehouse, that there may be food in my house. Test me in this, says the Lord almighty, and see if I will not throw open the floodgates of Heaven and pour out so much blessing that you will not have room enough for it.* (Malachi 3:10 NIV)

This is a very strong message coming directly from God. In this verse He is assuring us that it is all right to put Him to the test. In fact, in the Revised Standard Version, the same verse states, *Put me to the test says the Lord.* So, go ahead and put God to the test. If you are not presently giving your whole tithe, begin at once. The Scriptures relate that once you start giving God the amount that is due to Him first, there will be such an abundance of blessings guided your way that you will never want to stop tithing.

I read about a president of a large company who once said he had known many regular church-goers who, for one reason or another, stopped attending church, but he had never known anyone who stopped tithing once he had begun. Just talk to someone who tithes, and you will quickly learn that every tither is enthusiastic about tithing. They realize that our debt to God comes first and they enjoy pleasing Him.

Because this is a witness book I ask you: can we

WILL YOU PUT GOD TO THE TEST?

witness to others our belief in tithing? No one enjoys hearing another boasting about their increased wealth and finances and other blessings of life due to their tithing efforts. It is just not in order to tell others how God has blessed your life due to your commitment to tithing, but our witness to others must include this obligation. I am searching for the proper way to witness without giving people the impression that we are bragging about what God has done for us. With that fact in mind, we are told in the Scriptures that when we give, we are not to go running through the streets telling others about our giving. We are also forewarned that when we give, our left hand is not to know what the right hand is doing. To illustrate, here are Jesus' words on that point, *But when you give to the needy, do not let your left hand know what your right hand is doing, so that your giving may be in secret.· Then your Father, who sees what is done in secret will reward you.* (Matthew 6:3-4 NIV) So, how do we witness, being careful not to boast? Are we boasting when we tell others, "I am a tither"? I personally believe that it is pleasing to God to let it be known to others who might be strengthened in the faith by informing them that we obey God by giving our tithe to His work.

Another way I believe we can witness in this area is in the parenting of our children. ✝ Our children need to be informed that we follow what I often refer to as "the law of tithing."

✝ During conversation, at the proper time, mentioning to others that you believe in tithing and that you are a tither would be in good order and pleasing to God. It may be in good taste to add a statement such as, "I found out years ago that God's shovel is bigger than mine, and He will shovel more back to me than I can shovel His way."

Here's another way you may want to consider. ✝ If your relationship with the person you are speaking will allow, and if you do not mind being a bit aggressive, you may simply ask, "What do you think about giving a percentage of your earnings back to God?" It could lead into an interesting conversation that will allow you to witness by sharing your belief in tithing.

Prior to entering into any type of witness, you need to have available answers to questions which may result. It is my desire that this book will provide material that will prepare you for some of the questions that will be asked. Jesus stated facts about tithing

2000 years ago. He said, *Give and it will be given unto you; good measure, pressed down, shaken together, running over, will be put into your lap. For the measure you give will be the measure you get back.* (Luke 6:38 RSV)

Here is another quote that may interest you. Reverend Billy Graham has often said, "I dare you to try to outgive God."

During a sermon about giving, Reverend Robert Bogan pondered what happens when we refuse to give our tithes and offerings to God's work: "Does God take his share away from us anyway?" Reverend Bogan stated that he could not prove it Scripturally, but he almost could. Now that is something to discuss. What do you think about Reverend Bogan's statement?

Prior to closing this chapter, let's take a look at more Scripture related to the subject of giving:

- *When you help the poor you are lending to the Lord—and He pays wonderful interest on your loan.* (Proverbs 19:17 TLB)

- *He who shuts his ears to the cries of the poor will be ignored in his own time of need. (Proverbs 21:13 TLB)*

- *Honor the Lord by giving Him the first part of your income and he will fill your barns with wheat and barley and overflow your wine vats with the finest wines. (Proverbs 3:9-10 TLB)*

- *Jesus said it is more blessed to give than to receive. (Acts 20:35 NIV)*

- *Give and it shall be given unto you. (Luke 6:38 KJV)*

When tithing is discussed, almost always the question is asked, "Are we to give our tithes based on our net pay (after taxes) or on our gross pay (prior to taxes and deductions being taken out)?" When you ask a half dozen tithers that question, you will probably get a half dozen different opinions on the subject. Over the last few months, J.P. Patterson, our UPS delivery person, and I have been engaged in several conversations about tithing. He related to me what a person in his church Bible study group said on the subject of giving, prior to, and after taxes and deductions. He states, "I believe that if you give net tithes to God you will receive net rewards. If you give gross tithes, you will receive gross rewards."

Compared with the rest of this book, this chapter may contain the toughest of all ways to witness; but hang in there—as tough as it may seem, it will become easier and easier as your faith becomes stronger and stronger. Christianity is one of life's best-kept secrets, and within Christianity, giving to God's work is probably the best-kept secret. So, many of us go through our Christian lives enjoying many of God's blessings, while others receive special gifts and rewards because they have learned the joy of giving. God has more gifts awaiting us all if we will provide reasons for Him to give them to us. † If you are not a committed giver, I urge you to try it for six months. Put God to the test. After six months you can always make the decision to stop giving, but I do not believe you will.

CHAPTER 27
Wear a Cross

In an earlier chapter I detailed how we can witness by carrying a cross for Jesus. † Another way to witness is to wear a cross for Him. It is easy to do and I believe it makes a great impact on others.

Go to your Christian retail store and buy several small pin-on crosses. The size of the ones I like are about one-fourth inch high or slightly larger. The cost ranges from fifty cents to one dollar each. By purchasing several you will be able to attach them to several items of wearing apparel. I have known others to attach these crosses to suspenders, ball caps, belts, and wherever your imagination will lead you to place the crosses.

You may be thinking that many times people of little faith wear crosses on their clothing or personal attire. This is so true, but consider this: when a cross is worn, everyone who comes in view of the cross will be reminded that the cross is the symbol of our Lord and Savior. Over the years I have purchased many pin-on crosses, and I can assure you that people do notice them. † I have formed a habit of taking it off my clothing and giving it to the person that inquires about the cross. Most of the time, the person will exclaim, "Oh no, I don't want to take it; you are wearing it!" I then have the opportunity to further witness by telling him, "I really want you to have it. You see, I have dozens more pin-on crosses at my home. I love to give them to others who share my faith."

I have one cross I sometimes wear that is much larger than the pin-on I normally display. It is pearl white and stands out brightly when worn. On a number of occasions people have asked me, "Are you a preacher?" † I smile in such a way that their inquiry was a compliment, pause slightly, and answer them by saying, "No, I am not a preacher, but I am a disciple."

The same question is asked when I wear my Jesus belt buckles. Sometimes I seem to give them a slight shock when they learn I am not a pastor. I get the impression that they may be asking themselves, "Why would he be wearing a belt buckle with a picture of Jesus displayed on it if he is not a minister?"

You may discover, as I did, that wearing a small cross on an article of clothing will be an easy way for you to witness.

CHAPTER 28
Burma Shave

While growing up in the 1940s and '50s, I, along with millions of other people, was fascinated with those cute, rhyming Burma Shave signs that graced the highways back then. If you are not yet fifty, you may not even remember those signs. There would be a series of five or more signs mounted on posts spaced out along the highway that would allow the passengers to read the clever, amusing message as they motored down the highways or rural roads. The last signpost would contain the sponsor's product name. The shaving cream company paid the land owners rent on the space the signs occupied, and the American motorists loved those crazy, silly signs that were seen from coast to coast. One of my favorite Burma Shave signs was:

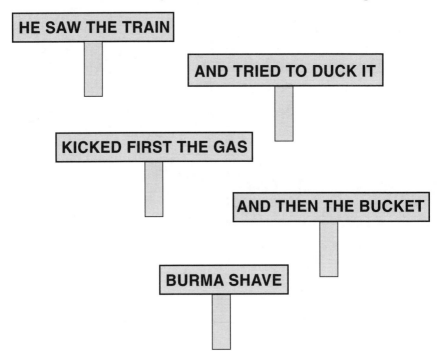

Here is another one I remember:

> **DRINKING DRIVERS**

> **NOTHING WORSE**

> **THEY PUT THE QUART**

> **BEFORE THE HEARSE**

> **BURMA SHAVE**

✝ I realize that we are now in the computer age, but I think it would be of much interest to have those signs appear again. Maybe the next time around the signs could have a Christian flavor with something like this:

> **THE WHALE PUT JONAH**

> **DOWN THE HATCH**

> **BUT COUGHED HIM UP**

> **BECAUSE HE SCRATCHED**

ROSES ARE RED

VIOLETS ARE BLUE

JESUS IS MY SAVIOR

HOW ABOUT YOU?

Or how about . . .

IF YOU THINK RELIGION

IS SUCH A BORE

JUST REMEMBER

WHO'S KEEPING SCORE

Is this a really wild idea or what? I know of no one who is involved in a sign project like this. As far as I know, it is an original idea. Perhaps some energetic group will see this as a witness project, and take it to the hilt.

CHAPTER 29
Lend a Hand!

Here is a method of witnessing that will, more-than-likely, assure you of a good night's sleep. † Take a look throughout your neighborhood, and choose someone who you believe has a need. Offer this person your assistance in some particular task that your neighbor wishes to have done, such as: painting a fence, yard work, house repairs, etc. With this assignment underway you will surely get to know this person better, and it may be the beginning of a beautiful friendship. Do not forget to get a nice plug in for the "King of Kings" and your salvation while working.

So, if you will take the time and you have the ability to lend a hand, this will be an easy way for you to witness. Be sure to take along your work gloves!

CHAPTER 30
Take Jesus for a Ride

In one chapter, I mentioned displaying a Bible on the dashboard of your vehicle as an easy way to witness. † Another related way to witness would be to purchase a statue of Jesus and mount it on the dashboard. Let Jesus ride along with you wherever you travel. I recently was browsing in one of those "everything is just a dollar" stores, and I came across a colorful figurine angel with golden wings mounted on a pedestal, standing six inches tall. The angel is now standing on the mantle of our family room. If you purchase such a statue, others will see it and know why it is there. The dollar store also had statues of Jesus, and I purchased one for my personal witness. It's a low-price item that won't set you back a lot; but wait, does this create a problem for you? With a Jesus statue on your automobile dashboard or sitting on your office desk, you may be somewhat concerned that some of your acquaintances may look at you a little strangely, and, perhaps, feel a little uncomfortable when you are witnessing your faith. We Christians are not ashamed of the Gospel, are we?

CHAPTER 31
It's Really Personal

Have you ever thought that you become a witness by your personal habits? Please take some time to give it your thoughts.

I was recently having breakfast at a Waffle House Restaurant near the Raleigh/Durham, North Carolina, Airport, and as I was paying and preparing to leave, I caught a glimpse of a gentleman who had a large open Bible on the counter. He was in conversation with the man next to him. I quietly walked over and excused myself by saying, "Please pardon me, but I could not leave without remarking to you that your light was shining for others to see." I then thumped his open Bible with my finger. He smiled and thanked me for taking the time to speak to him, and stated, "This is the most important book ever printed."

Folks are very observant of our personal habits, the places we go, whom we are with, and the things we do. ✝ We are always witnessing to others with our personal habits even though we may not even be aware of it.

People watch where we go, what we say, and what we do. To those of us who profess the Christian life, whether we know it or not, our reputation is on the line every minute of every day. All of us have short-comings, and we are all sinners, but God loves us anyway. He hates sin, but He loves the sinner. I have found that in my Christian walk my personal habits improve as I walk closer with God.

CHAPTER 32
Envelope Witness

Did you ever stop and think just how many persons may see an envelope that is mailed from your home or office from the time it leaves your hands until it reaches the person to whom it is addressed? Do this: look in one of those mail order catalogs that offers address labels. You will find that you can purchase five hundred address labels for anywhere from two to five dollars. Most labels offer four-line printing. † Use three lines for your name and address, and, here's the kicker: use the fourth line to proclaim God's glory by adding a line that will witness to all who see it. The line could be as simple as *God loves you,* or you could design your own tag line. If you have envelopes printed for business or home use, you may add your witness message anywhere you so desire, in as many words or as large as you want your witness to be.

Viggo Christensen, from New York State, has been a customer of our company for more than twenty years.

Viggo Christensen
Schenectady, NY

U.S. Postage

JESUS IS LORD!

Empire Publishing
PO Box 717
Madison NC 27025-0717

I can always identify his correspondence as I rifle through the morning's mail, as written crudely, and in big bold letters across the envelope are the following words, "**JESUS IS LORD**." This is Viggo's way of witnessing by way of the U.S. Postal Service.

✝ Believe me when I tell you that a large handwritten message across the envelope has quite an impact when received. I remembered! I wonder how many others have also remembered? Will you begin an envelope witness for your Lord and Savior today? Try it. God will surely bless you for your effort.

CHAPTER 33
A Blessing Missed?

Ten years ago a Christian family I know got to pondering about the true meaning of Christmas. Their thoughts rambled from how to direct their attention more towards the celebration of the birthday of Jesus and less about giving the proper gift to everyone on their Christmas gift list. After much discussion and thought, here is what they decided: † "This year instead of giving gifts to everyone, we will give to the needy, the same amount of money allotted for gifts." Sounds great, huh? It did sound like a great idea—just what they thought Jesus would want them to do. So they got out the list of people (children excluded) who routinely receive a Christmas present from them, and the following letter was mailed to everyone on their list.

Dear _____,

Over the past few years, we have discovered that Christmas has become a time to "get through" rather than a time to savor and appreciate. Perhaps our expanding family has contributed to making the get-ready time more frenzied than it was in the past.

Of course, the seasonal contacts with you—whether by telephone, in person, or through an exchange of gifts—always brings us joy. When the season comes to a close, though, we can't help but wonder if our mode of celebration pleases God and reflects the real significance of Christmas.

In most cases, none of us are truly in need of material things, and our spiritual lives may be less full than they could be. One way to enrich our spiritual lives is to extend a helping hand to others. As your gift to us in this coming Christmas, would you consider making a gift of your time, your talent, or your money to someone or some group in need? The only request we make is that you tell us about the gift you have given. In return, we propose to make a similar gift to you. This Christmas season, we have elected to give our time, money, and support to our County Unit of Good News Jail and Prison Ministries.

The purpose of the Chaplaincy program at the County Jail is to encourage men and women toward rehabilitation through the regenerative power of Jesus Christ. This central spiritual role is matched by a responsibility to social needs. The primary goal of this ministry is restoration of those incarcerated, spiritually and socially. This program at the jail is open to the daily population of over 100 inmates as well as the more than 5,000 inmates who pass through the jail each year. The primary focus is on the inmates, yet the ministry includes outreach to jail staff members and the families of those incarcerated.

The benefits of this type of giving at Christmas come in the fact that the prisoners will know that someone cares about them, especially at this season which is probably the loneliest time of the year for them.

The plain facts are that incarceration does not work. Approximately ninety-five percent of all inmates will be released back into the community. Unfortunately, about eighty percent of all released inmates will be incarcerated again.

The Good News Jail and Prison Ministries is an international jail and prison ministry which provides institutional chaplains. It is a recognized leader in jail and prison chaplaincy work and is the largest supplier of civilian jail and prison chaplains. The objective of the chaplaincy is to provide a local pastoral ministry that is committed to spiritual and social restoration. To achieve that goal, Good News Jail and Prison Ministries places trained ordained men as staff Chaplains who provide a comprehensive ministry to the inmates, their families, and the institutional staff.

Please think about the above for a while, and let us have your reactions and suggestions. We want to know what you think, even if you've completed your shopping!

We love you all dearly and will respect whatever you decide to do. Our major concern is that we refocus our efforts toward a more meaningful celebration of the birth of Jesus Christ.

Love,

From Our Family

This, of course, is looked upon as another way we may witness to others, but did the message get through to the mail receivers? Were the receivers appreciative that the money was given to the needy in their names instead of the gift normally received? It saddens me to report that the majority did not even give the couple the courtesy of even a mention or a thank you for their efforts. The substitution was not appreciated, and they felt afterwards that some probably thought the gesture was an excuse not to give Christmas presents. I surmised that most people thought that giving to the needy at Christmas time was a good idea, but when it came down to them not receiving or giving personal gifts, it was not something the majority wanted to do.

While reading the letter, the message comes through to me that Christ is the reason we celebrate Christmas. We, as Christians, should give to the glory of God. I am of the opinion that those families that did not appreciate the gifts given by the Christian couple truly missed a blessing that Christmas season.

CHAPTER 34
It's Personal

As I have mentioned elsewhere in this book, while driving across the country I especially enjoy reading personalized license plates of other travelers. You can really see some peculiar ones. Some are confusing; some are cute; and some are impossible to comprehend. There are license tags that have initials, names, nicknames, places, things, and whatever the human mind can demise. As the traffic whizzes by, I have the opportunity to read almost all personalized license plates.

Perhaps, I should state my position on my driving habits on our highway system. My wife of almost forty years, Noreen, absolutely will not exceed the posted speed limit, and I rarely will exceed the posted speed by more than five miles per hour. Therefore, we spend the majority of our interstate driving time in the right lane. You have seen the many signs displayed along the roadsides that read, *Slower traffic keep right.* Well, that is what we named ourselves: "slower traffic;" so, I am able to read many personalized vehicle license plates as the faster traffic passes us by.

Besides the majority of tags that poke fun at this or that, tell who loves whom, and so on, every once in a while some driver will zip by bearing a spiritual message that is witnessing to every pair of eyes that views the tag. I wish I had written down all that I have seen. However, I do remember some that I will share with you.

While driving through a busy street in Charlotte, North Carolina, I spied a car that had the message, *John 14:14.* That evening I was anxious to learn what that driver was witnessing to me. My hotel Bible revealed that John 14:14 (KJV) reads, *If ye shall ask anything in my name I will do it.* I wondered how many others who read that tag looked up the Scripture as I did.

In High Point, North Carolina, there is an auto running around town with a personalized license plate that reads, *YES TO GOD.* Other personalized license plates that have been used by people to witness their salvation include: *JESUS #1, GOD CAN, RUSAVED, TRUSTHIM, TRY GOD,* and *BLESS U.*

Spotted on a special-ordered license plate, while driving around town in Madison, North Carolina, the plate lays out a simple witness that reads, *LOVE GOD.*

What personalized license plates have you seen that are witnesses? Please take a moment to write us, and we may include them in a future updated version of this book. † If you are searching for a way that you may witness, give the personalized license plate consideration. It's truly an easy way to witness.

CHAPTER 35

Other License Plates

•*Buckle up with Jesus.*
•*God bless America.*
•*God is my co-pilot.*
•*Jesus saves.*
•*See you in church on Sunday.*

I have seen these license tags on cars and trucks running back and forth across our wonderful country. They appear mostly on the front, as the vast majority of state license plates require only one license tag, and, of course, they are required to be placed on the rear of the vehicle. For most of us drivers, that leaves the front license plate area wide open to place a department store or flea market-type plate on our vehicle.

Let me see now...how about a plate that reads *Chevrolet #1 in U.S.A.*, or something such as *If you can't run with the big dogs—stay on the porch.* Or how about this: † Pick out a tag that will allow others to know exactly how you feel about your salvation. There are many selections from which you can choose. When they see your vehicle, there will be no doubt as to exactly where you stand on the subject of your conviction.

You may choose from one of the following:
•*Christt is the answer.*
•*One way ♦ Jesus*
•*Smile, God loves you.*
•*The Lord is my shepherd.*
•*Prayer helps.*
•*Jesus saves.*
•*Jesus never fails.*
•*God bless our flag.*

You may be shaking your head saying, "I really do

not feel the calling to place a tag on the front of my car telling the world I am a Christian." If, for any reason, you would not feel comfortable advertising for Jesus, you need to pause and seek God's guidance. I feel sure that you will know in your heart what the right decision is. *We are not trying to please men but God, who tests our hearts.* (I Thessalonians 2:4b)

On my personal automobile, I have a flea market especially made license plate that bears the identity of my home state and across the plate in large blue letters reads this simple message: *Try God.* It was custom made for me at a flea market near Garden City, a resort area near Myrtle Beach, South Carolina. The cost was little, but the rewards have been many. I take that message everywhere I go—to restaurants, the bank, post office, etc. I see folks looking at the front of my automobile, and a few times people have remarked, "I like your license plate."

My all-time favorite license tag is the one that was mounted on the front of a conversion travel van. As you can see, the tag asks a couple of questions. Do you believe? Can you see? Between the two statements is what to some may appear to be a jumbled-up nothing, but to others, the name *JESUS* stands out. Can you see the name of Jesus? Keep looking, and His name will appear.

My wife's car has a front license plate that shows an automobile key, and the message reads, *Jesus Christ, your key to salvation.* So, my fellow Christian, please heed my advice; as you acquired this book, I assume, to learn easy ways to witness. What could be easier than attaching a witness message to the front or your car, truck, motor home, or whatever? It takes such little effort, and these type license plates are very affordable.

Do you ever get the feeling that God is testing you? Are you being tested right now? If this is a test, will you pass or fail?

CHAPTER 36
Just Let Things Happen!

You and I are very much aware that when we came to know the Lord, things began to happen. As followers of Christ, it is our duty to tell others about the happenings. Part of my testimony is what happened in my life when I became a follower.

First, I was forgiven of all my past sins. *Unto Him that loved us, and washed us from our sins in His own blood.* (Revelation 1:5 KJV)

My old nature was instantly changed. *Therefore, if any man be in Christ, he is a new creature. Old things are passed away; behold all things become new.* (II Corinthians 5:17 KJV)

The power of Satan was broken away from me. *To open their eyes and to turn them from darkness to light and from the power of Satan unto God.* (Acts 26:18 KJV)

No longer did I have the fear of death, as the fear was removed. *And free those who all their lives were held in slavery by their fear of death.* (Hebrews 2:15 KJV)

I instantly became a member in the family of God. *To all who received Him, to those that believed in His name, He gave the right to become children of God.* (John 1:12 KJV)

I then found a purpose for my life that had true meaning like I had never before experienced. *I have come that they may have life and that they may have it more abundantly.* (John 10:10 KJV)

† Tell others if you have experienced the same happenings in your life. Things do happen when you come to Jesus Christ.

CHAPTER 37
I Saw You Do It

When you are out in the world and you come upon someone who has a salvation message or saying printed on his T-shirt, hat, or other wearing apparel, have you ever thought, here is a fellow Christian proclaiming to all who see it that he or she is saved and wants everyone to know it?

How about if, while on your way home from work, you stop by a quick service store to pick up some needed item, and there it is in the parking lot right next to your automobile—a pickup truck with a license tag on the front that reads in big red letters, *Trust in the Lord.*

Or, suppose you are zooming down the highway, and you exit quickly to refuel. As you pull up to the pumps your attention focuses on the large flagpole in front of the gas station pumps. It has a colorful flag waving in the breeze, but it is not a regular type of flag that is seen so often—this flag has the face of Jesus on the side nearest the post and written in red on the outer side are the precious words, *Jesus loves you!*

On down the road you are elevating yourself up a long incline, and you make preparation to pass a beat-up older van when you notice this sign that has a simple message, *Honk if you love Jesus.* That is your invitation to give your horn a little tap, and, when passing, you could give the driver a little wave and smile to compliment his witness. Or, you could simply pass the vehicle and make no effort to acknowledge the witness. The choice is yours!

† The message that is being projected in this brief chapter is: when you see others proclaiming the gospel of Jesus Christ, give them a pat on the back. Compliment them on their witness. This will encourage them to continue their witness.

CHAPTER 38
Just by *Not* Doing

Almost everything in this book contains things that we do to witness to others, but how often do we share our faith by *not* doing? Reflecting on that thought, I was bombarded with thoughts about hundreds of ways Christians witness every day by *not* doing.

We could begin with the Ten Commandments. † Each one contains the words, *Thou shall **not** ...* One might say that people witness by *not* attending places that would not be pleasing to their family or God. † A recovering alcoholic may share his faith by *not* consuming strong drink. † Teenagers may be strong witnesses when they do *not* involve their lives with drugs.

Christians are watched carefully. People watch what we do, where we go, what we say, what we eat, where we live, what we wear, and even whom we are with. Some are watching with the thought of seeing us betray our faith, and, sometimes we do betray our God and our faith. Hey—Christians are not perfect, just SAVED!

The ways of witnessing to our faith by not doing are many. Think about it! What can you *not* do that would be a witness to those who see and know you? If you take the time you will be able to compile a long list of ways to witness by *not* doing. Your assignment here, should you decide to accept the challenge, would be to write down the ways you can witness by *not* doing! Keep your witness active just by *not* doing.

CHAPTER 39
Invite People to Church

Giving invitations for people to attend church may sound like a pretty standard statement. Let me put you in the spotlight by asking you just when was the last time you did invite a friend, neighbor, relative, or co-worker to join you at your church for a weekly worship service? Has it been so long that you do not even remember? If you are like many of us, weeks may have passed since you have invited someone to join you at church.

You would not want to be in the percentage of Christians that *have never* invited anyone, would you? You know the answer to that question! God knows the answer. Work it out to satisfy your own self. I have heard it said and have said it myself, "People know where the church is located. They pass by its door often. If they want to attend our church, they will."

Of course, that is a foolish statement for anyone to say or believe. I believe we are required by God's word to invite others to attend activities at our church. So, if you are involved in a church environment where you are happy and pleased; and you feel the Spirit of God within, then invite others to attend your house of worship where you may share the blessings you have obtained.

Noreen and I stopped by a friend's house one afternoon. As we drove down the long driveway, our eyes fell upon a flashy, new sports car just about ready to leave as we were driving in. Alongside the car was our friend, Ronnie Webster, saying good-bye to the young couple in the car as they were preparing to leave. Ronnie's head quickly turned as he saw us approaching; his eyes lit up, and a smile came over his face. He was showing us how glad he was to see us. As I was walking up the driveway, Ronnie was finalizing his visit with the young couple by inviting them to worship with him the next Sunday. † He yelled out, "Come down to my church Sunday; we would surely be pleased to have you." The young man exclaimed, "I haven't lost a thing in church. That's not for me!"

Although I never discussed it with Ronnie, I would surmise that it was not the first time he had invited the young couple to church, and knowing him as I do, he will probably ask the young man and his girlfriend again at the next opportune time. Ronnie's witness was out there standing tall for us and the young couple to see. When the young man belted out that church was not for him and that he had not *lost* a thing in church, my mind gave off the thought waves that *he could find* a thing or two at church if he would just attend sometime.

† I know a minister who pastors two churches in Sandy Ridge, North Carolina, and she goes about witnessing in a different way from most people. While the majority of us church members invite people to come to church, Reverend Evelyn Browning goes out into the homes, businesses, and other places of the world for the purpose of leading them to the Lord. Once they are converted to Christianity, she then informs the new in Christ about the importance of being part of the gathering of God's people known as the church. Since this new birth of evangelism became a part of Evelyn's ministry, she has averaged bringing salvation to six converts each month. When I spoke with her in January she revealed that with the assistance of her church evangelistic group, they expect to exceed one hundred converts this year. Evangelism works. Its efforts bring the lost to Christ. In less than one year, the Snow Hill Methodist members have seen their attendance almost double from approximately 80 regulars to an average of 150 per Sunday. Based on her performance thus far, I know her estimate of one hundred will be met, and, in all likelihood, will be

greatly exceeded. Her methods of going after the un-churched has led her to become "on fire," winning the lost to the Lord. This young, vibrant minister is a powerful soldier in God's army. In fact, I predict she will prove herself worthy to be put into a higher position of leading fellow clergymen and church groups as she teaches them how to evangelize her way. † As easy as it is, we *are* witnessing to others when we invite others to attend worship at our church.

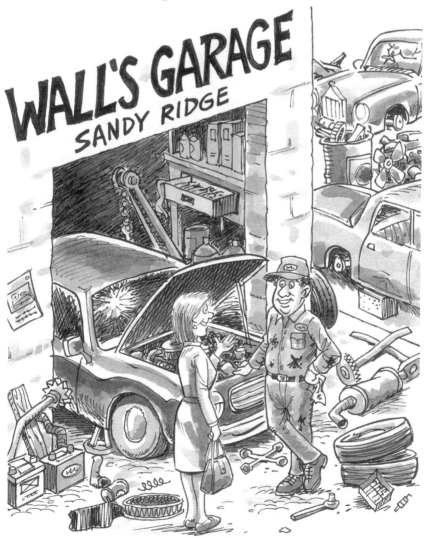

My car is O.K. I just stopped by to talk about the Lord.

CHAPTER 40
Go and Worship

Have you ever thought that you are witnessing when you attend a church worship service? Just think about it. † Your church friends, neighbors, and acquaintances with whom you come in contact are aware that you are a church-attending person. That, in itself, is a strong form of witnessing. If we attend worship services without sharing and expressing our faith as we go down life's road, we leave a lot of questions with those who observe us. We may even lead people to think that we are hypocrites.

Do you believe that, if we are followers of Christ we *will* attend church on a regular schedule for our own personal salvation and to show others we need the church? Based on my experience, regular church attendance is like being hooked up to a battery charger; by the time six days roll by my batteries have a tendency to become weak, and a Sunday morning worship service is just what I need to get myself charged up to carry me through the next week.

We are reminded to *Come, kneel before the Lord our Maker, for He is our God.* (Psalm 95:6-7 TLB) In the book of John it is written, *For it's not where we worship that counts, but how we worship—is our worship spiritual and real?* (John 4:21-23 TLB) Throughout the Bible God's words instruct followers to worship and give Him praise and glory. Our real spirituality shines through whether we are in a physical building known as a church, or in the world away from the church. However, attending a local church gives us an attachment on which we may establish a home base for our salvation.

If you are not now established with a local church, and you are interested in gaining strength in your witness, you may gain extra strength by attending worship services on a regular basis.

CHAPTER 41
Write and Visit Prisoners

I have always had a lot of compassion for those unfortunate individuals who have had their freedom removed and are incarcerated behind the bars of jails and prisons. The majority of inmates are there because they have broken man's laws, but God's law to Christians indicates that, regardless of the reason they are there, we are to love them and be concerned for their souls. It is my belief that if we witness to them perhaps their lives will be changed, and when they return to society, a better life will be awaiting them.

As Christians, we are aware that it may very well mean that if they accept Jesus as their personal Savior, never again will they return to their past life; they will know that God will surely provide them with an eternal life when the timc comes for them to leave this earth.

How may we help them? How may we become a witness and guide them through their time of *discontentment*? Before we can do anything, we must have their trust. They must believe that we are sincere and are truly interested in them as individuals. We must not show signs of pitying them for where they are. They know where they are and why they are there.

† A good way to start is to search out someone who is behind bars, get an address, and write to him. Ask fellow church members, business associates, or acquaintances for someone's name to whom you may write. You don't need to know a lot about his background. He may be willing to tell you much about himself and will possibly answer your letter. I've been told that inmates look forward to receiving mail. In fact, I would suspect that mail call is the highlight of their day.

If you are not able to come up with a person to whom you may write, phone your sheriff's department. Ask to speak to the jailer; he should be able to give you the name of an inmate who would benefit from receiving mail. If you contact a county, state, or federal prison, you would direct your inquiry to the warden's office.

When contact is made and the inmate writes to you,

the door will be opened wide for you to begin your witness. I am sure you will not have any problem choosing topics for your letters. Just ask about his family, hobbies, his line of work on the outside and whatever the Lord leads you to write about. I'm sure what you need to say will be revealed to you. ✝ A follow-up to this witness after a few letters have been exchanged is to arrange to visit him on visiting day. This is an inexpensive way to witness to others; and it is so easy I hope many will join in with this ministry. Just remember God loves them and wants them in his fold.

CHAPTER 42
Have a Testamint

While I was gathering some thoughts for this book, my wife Noreen came into my office area exclaiming, "I bought something for you today," and she displayed two packages of mints. One was flavored spearmint, and the other package was peppermint.

I welcomed the mints, and upon close examination, I was pleased to learn that these were not the regular run-of-the-mill candy mints. The name that spanned the length spelled out the name, *TESTAMINTS!* Turning the "testamints" package on its side, I found a Bible verse. It displayed the following: *Be kind and compassionate to one another, forgiving each other, just as in Christ God forgave you.* (Ephesians 4:32 NIV)

WOW! Here is a brand new product on the market that proclaims the Gospel of Jesus so well. They are lightweight, will fit nicely into a pocket, and each package will give Christians the opportunity to witness twelve times. I could not wait to tear open the package to see and taste the contents. The "testamints" are square-shaped, and right in the middle of the mint, a cross is indented there on both sides.

What a novel idea: buy candy mints that freshen your breath, taste good (For weight watchers, one mint has a mere 5 calories.), and gives you the opportunity to witness. They are available at Christian bookstores and other locations. Ask for them. I hope you will be as impressed with them as I was. It is another easy way to witness.

If this idea gets your attention, go for it. ✝ Include witnessing with "testamints" as part of your salvation witness. If this idea seems too laid back, perhaps you may consider the next avenue for witnessing—by giving folks chocolate candy bars.

CHAPTER 43
Sweet Tidings

In the same store that sold "Testamints" were gourmet milk chocolate candy bars that carried spiritual messages on a royal blue outside wrapper. They were manufactured by the Sweet Tidings Company of Roeland Park, Kansas 66205. One had the message printed, *Thinking of you; I thank my God upon every remembrance of you.* (Phil. 1:3)

The other chocolate bar was gold-colored and in large letters was the message, *God bless you*, with smaller print noting that there is a message inside the wrapper. Upon opening the wrapper carefully, the following message was revealed:

You ought to know who Jesus is: *(John 3:16 NIV) For God so loved the world that he gave his one and only son, that whoever believes in Him shall not perish but have eternal life.*

Why Jesus came: *(Romans 5:8 NIV) But God demonstrates His own love for us in this: while we were still sinners, Christ died for us.*

What Jesus said: *(Revelation 3:20 NIV) Here I am! I stand at the door and knock. If anyone hears my voice and opens the door, I will come in.*

How Jesus saves: *(Romans 10:9-10 NIV) That if you confess with your mouth Jesus is Lord, and believe in your heart that God raised Him from the dead, you shall be saved; for with the heart, man believes, resulting in righteousness, and with the mouth he confesses, resulting in salvation.*

Don't deny God the right to be Lord of our life. Receive Jesus Christ today. Unfortunately, without God, doing things our own way we sin. When we trust in God and yield to Him, we are brought into the family of God. Seek a Bible believing church.

God Bless You,
Sweet Tidings, Inc.

✝ If your budget will allow it, you may want to pick up several candy bars and do some easy witnessing armed with gourmet chocolate in hand.

CHAPTER 44
Bible in Hotels

Because of my interest in movies, every year or so I plan an excursion to southern California for the purpose of seeking out and visiting the rocks, hills, ranches, and various locations where many films were made. On my last trip, I met ten friends from various parts of the east coast who gathered with me in California. In addition to staying on the trail visiting movie locations, we were able to spend some time with many film stars including the "King of the Cowboys" himself, Roy Rogers; Robert Blake, star of the *Baretta* TV show; several folks from one of my favorite TV shows— *The Andy Griffith Show:* Don Knotts, Betty Lynn (Thelma Lou), everyone's favorite, Howard Morris (Ernest T. Bass); among others.

Now that I have briefly explained why I was in Hollywood, I will get to the reason for including this chapter in the book. I shared a room with a long time friend from the state of Florida, Sherman Pippin. When we checked into the room, Sherman looked in the night stand drawer, removed the Bible and placed it on top of the night stand, next to the telephone. The next morning prior to leaving out for our day of fun and adventure, he placed a dollar bill on top of the Bible. † He explained that by placing the money on top of the Bible, the cleaning person's eyes would focus on the money and the Bible. To him that was his way of witnessing to her. This may seem like a trivial type of witness, but it was important to Sherman. As a result, it became a witness to me as the Bible remained there on the night stand, in our daily view, during our eight day stay at the Beverly Garland Holiday Inn Hotel. † Another thought occurred to me when our stay was over: Sherman left the Bible out on the night stand, which meant that the cleaning lady would be required to take the Holy book in her hands and return it to its place in the drawer as she prepared our room for its next guests.

If you have other thoughts regarding how we could witness while staying in hotels, I would be interested in knowing your ideas. Just write and tell us. Who knows? It may be a witness suggestion that will be printed in an updated version of *Let Your Light Shine.*

CHAPTER 45
Give a Pen

As a business owner for twenty-five years, I am constantly seeking ways to promote sales and keep our company's name before the buying public. One way I have found successful is to purchase advertising specialties that have our company's name printed on them, such as key chains, ball caps, calendars, etc. We have found that the public appreciates being given these ad items.

An item that we use more than anything else is ball point pens. They are items used daily by almost everyone. While doing research for this book, the idea came to me: What a neat and effective way to witness to others! † You could purchase pens in quantity, have a witness message printed on the pens, and give them to people with whom you come in contact as you travel through this world.

The message could be as simple as, "God loves you," or it could be a message used to invite others to church. You may want to have one of your church groups take on the pen witness project. Pens can be purchased for as low as twenty-five cents each making the cost for a hundred ball point pens to be in the price range of twenty-five to thirty-five dollars.

Almost everyone will readily accept ball point pens. Specially engraved pens tell others that you are a Christian and you are following God's words by witnessing. "How can these advertising pens be acquired?" you may ask. Look in your telephone yellow pages under advertising or advertising specialties. Phone one or more advertising specialty agencies and compare prices and pen quality.

A few years ago, I discovered a pen specialty company that offers, what I believe to be, a good quality pen at a very reasonable price. I have used their ad pens for about five years. You may phone National Pen Company at 1-888-672-8825, and ask for Ms. Lee Clark. She will assist you with choosing a low-cost pen. Pens are a welcomed give-away item and should fit most budgets.

CHAPTER 46
Visit Nursing Homes

Health care facilities are always on the lookout for ways to keep their patients involved with worthwhile projects and keep them entertained. Consider this: Phone or visit a local nursing home or hospital and request permission to visit those within the facility. Our church organizes a Bingo gathering each month where some members go to the nursing home and gather a group of patients together for the purpose of playing Bingo games with prizes awarded to the winners. (Everyone who participates in playing always wins a prize.)

† Perhaps you may get permission to stroll down

the halls and visit with those who wish to be visited. You may desire to take along some home-baked cookies, or if you play a musical instrument and/or sing, you may want to give of your talent and bring a little happiness to those who will appreciate your time and talent. To those who wish to have a conversation, that would be a wonderful time for you to share your faith and allow them the opportunity to share theirs.

You will have a very captive audience, and nursing home patients, most often, can never have too much company. How about it? Is this an easy witness for you? If it is, go ahead and make that phone call today!

CHAPTER 47
Write the Rich and Famous

As Christians, we are commanded to be most interested and concerned about others regardless of their status in this life—even those famous persons whose names are known throughout the world. They are in a position (unlike most people) to carry their faith into concerts, films, television and radio broadcasts, newspapers, magazines, fan mail, and other forms of the mass media.

I believe that celebrities who take the time to tell their fans and others about their faith in God will be blessed in many ways. Perhaps after reading this chapter, those famous celebrities who make it their policy *not* to bring God into their public lives will give consideration to professing their faith in future public appearances.

I was saddened recently when I watched a glamorous superstar of movies, television and the music industry, being interviewed on late-night television. She strongly professed her faith in God several times during the interview and spoke of her faith, including how she based her career and her life on heavenly things. The interviewer moved into a made-for-TV movie segment in which the musical-actor had portrayed an angel who had been assigned back on earth to assist her guardian angel with a special heavenly assignment. While being quizzed about her portrayal of an angel, the entertainment headliner convincingly proclaimed that playing the role of the angel may be as close as she would ever get to heaven. The doubt in her voice led her to further her statements by adding in a somber way, "I hope I make it to heaven, but I'm not so sure." At that moment the thought came to me, how sad! Here is a wealthy, famous entertainer who is reported to have worldly assets in excess of 500 million dollars, but she is not even sure if heaven will be her eternal home. This lady is very intelligent, a good business woman, and seems quite knowledgeable about God's word. I can only assume that she may not be sure of her relationship with God. I am only assuming that fact, not judging her.

God says in order to go to heaven you must be born again. In John 3:7 KJV, Jesus said to Nicodemus, *Ye must be born again.* His plan is simple: you must realize you are a sinner—*for all have sinned and come short of the glory of God.* (Romans 3:23 KJV) God's remedy for sin is that we confess to Him that we are sinners and that His son, our Lord Jesus Christ, died for our sins. The next step is we simply ask Jesus to come into our lives, *for whosoever shall call upon the name of the Lord shall be saved.* (Romans 10:13 KJV) Jesus said, *Behold I stand at the door and knock; if any man* (person) *hear my voice and open the door I will come in to him.* (Revelation 3:20 KJV)

After taking these steps, we simply take God at His word and claim His salvation by faith. Believe, and we will be saved. No church affiliation, being a good person, or performing good works, can save us. God does the saving. We may say that it cannot be that simple. Yes it can! It is Scriptural. It is God's plan. God's power will save you, keep you saved, and enable you to live a victorious Christian life.

When we see or hear famous people make statements about not knowing whether or not they will make it through the gates of glory, how should we Christians react? † One way would be to take the time and write a letter to the person, proclaiming God's love for us all. Your witness letter may make a change in the celebrity's life, assuring him of his destiny.

CHAPTER 48
Use this Book

Elsewhere within these pages, I have informed you that I am not a minister. I cannot preach. I have tried on a few occasions to teach a Sunday school class without much success. I am not a good teacher, and to those professional writers and literature scholars, the evidence is very clear that one of my talents is not writing; but with God's help and the assistance of wife, family, friends, pastors, and others this book has become a reality. My Bible knowledge, also, is limited; but I know absolutely for sure that God has given me, as He has given you, a talent or talents to use to glorify His name.

✝ Perhaps one of your God-given talents may be using this book in your witness. If this is of interest, you have probably discovered ways to use it that appeal to you. I have a few suggestions as to how you may use the book to witness to others.

First, read the book through two or three times. It won't take much time. When you feel comfortable with the contents, take the book with you wherever you go. ✝ When the opportunity arises and you find yourself in the company of others, during your conversation, pull the book out and exclaim, "Look at the book I am now reading, *Let Your Light Shine*. To my knowledge, there is not another book similar to it anywhere. There is one chapter that was of particular interest to me," etc. At that time, and if you feel that you have the attention of the person or persons in your group, go ahead and refer them to the chapter that was of special interest to you. Ask them for their thoughts. Get some feedback. Say, "I am really interested in what you have to say on this particular subject."

Remember, the purpose of this book is to remind

us to tell others about Christ. Show it to others. If you can show others your interest in this easy witness book, perhaps they will have interest in owning a copy, so it will be available at their homes or offices. That will allow them the opportunity to pass it along to others. † Another way the book can be used is to buy several copies, and write or type a label that reads:

Please accept this book with my best wishes. After you read it, don't shelf it and allow it to gather dust. Pass it along to others.

CHAPTER 49
Hero Belt Buckles

I like to wear western-style clothing. I have always been an admirer of the western duds and accessories, and I suppose I always will. I have the hats, vests, jeans, boots, ties, coats, and the adornments that go along with the clothing. I almost always wear a western belt. I have narrow ones and some with silver ornaments, but I especially like fancy belt buckles.

While browsing through a large flea market near Pigeon Forge, Tennessee, I came across a belt buckle that had a circle frame where a silver dollar could be mounted, but this one was different. Instead of a coin, there was a colorful, round photograph of Jesus. I made a quick decision to purchase it, telling the vendor, "I want this buckle. How much?" How about that, I thought, here is another *easy way to witness*! † I wear this buckle a lot, and what fun I have had wearing it. Folks continuously admire the buckle and comment about it. When folks comment on the Jesus buckle, I thank them for noticing and quickly exclaim, † "He's my hero!" People often ask me where they can buy one like it.

One of the Jesus buckles I have at present measures approximately three inches wide by two inches high. The other buckle is smaller and is designed for a smaller belt. It measures approximately one and one-half inches high.

Ladies, also, can join in on this easy witness method.

I plan to give some Jesus buckles for gifts in the future. Perhaps you will consider the same. Do you know of a more meaningful gift you could give someone for Christmas or another occasion?

If you are interested in acquiring Jesus buckles and

cannot locate one in your area, you may mail a self addressed stamped envelope to the publisher, and information as to where you may purchase one will be promptly sent your way.

CHAPTER 50
Bless the Storks

As disciples of Christ, we are to seek out those who have not been washed in the lamb's blood of life and witness to them. When a friend or neighbor is blessed with the arrival of a newborn baby, that event allows us Christians a golden opportunity to share our faith with the new parents.

When babies are born, friends, neighbors, and relatives surround the newborn with life's necessities by pouring out gifts. † This would be an opportune time to give the child a children's Bible. It could be engraved with gold letters containing the child's name, and the Bible may become a valued gift through the years.

When you give the children's Bible, I would suggest you fill out the information page with details about the child, and where you fill out the space for your name, you could add, *from: (your names), your Chris-*

tian friends.

Have you ever heard of giving a Bible to a newborn? Why not? I believe it would be a welcomed gift to the parents, and, in years to come, appreciated by the child.

CHAPTER 51
Place a Tract Rack

† If you are a business owner, it would be a very easy task to make space available in your workplace for a neat and orderly rack that would house Christian literature. The rack would be there as a witness that someone at your establishment loves the Lord and wishes to share salvation with others.

Okay, so you are not a business owner. Should that stop you from arranging to have Christian literature racks placed in business establishments? I would suspect that you have Christian friends who are owner-operators of businesses—namely restaurants, quick food stores, motorcycle shops, automobile repair shops, furniture stores, or the like! Now, the wheels in your brain should be turning out prospective business owners who would probably permit you space in their Christian business operation to place a tract rack. Before any worthwhile project gets very far along, the question that surely must be asked is, "Hey! How much would it cost to buy and stock such a rack?" The next questions probably will be, "Where can I acquire the literature at an affordable price?" and, "What would I need to start up a project like this?"

One good source for buying religious tracts and similar items is a company that conducts a worldwide mail order business out of the state of Texas. They have a large selection of gospel tracts and those little Bibles that are so popular. My pastor friend, Bill Lovings, prefers the small Bibles for giveaways because, he says, "Folks won't throw away the tiny Bibles like they will tracts." Like the tracts, the Bibles cost only a few cents each. Bill buys a thousand or more of them at a time and enjoys the high volume discount.

To inquire about the products offered and their prices, write: Sowers of Seed, Box 6217, Ft. Worth, Texas 76115.

CHAPTER 52
Show Your Pearly Whites

Christians should be the happiest people this side of glory. So how about letting the world be aware of the joy in our lives by spreading those rosy cheeks, and show those pearly white teeth? Plain and simple:
† Give the world a smile each day.

Most of us would be in agreement that in or-der for our Christian witness to be effective, we must project the im-age that we Christians are happy with our sal-vation; we need to smile just as much as our faith will permit.

Of course, no one likes a phony; our smile must be genuine. It's pretty easy to spot in-sincerity, especially in one's personality. It sounds simple enough —all that is necessary to witness to our faith is to smile.

Do you know what transpires when we give some-one a smile? Chances are that person will give one right back to you.

CHAPTER 53
Check it Out!

Has the thought ever passed through your brain cells that your personal checking account can be a form of witness? † Consider this: in the upper left side of your personal checks where your name, address, phone number, drivers license number and other vital information appear, there is ample space to have a spiritual saying or Bible verse printed.

For your easy witness consideration, here is a sample personal check:

Jean Roberts	No. 216
210 Main Street	
Anytown, USA 00000	Date_May 1, 1998_
Phone 555-2029	
May God Bless You this Day!	

Pay to the order of _____Public Drug Store_____ $ 17.16

Seventeen dollars and 16/100-——————————————————Dollars

Bank of Salvation
Heavens Gates, Over There

For _Notions_   Jean Roberts

:21110255:3412 87661234

CHAPTER 54
Quote Scriptures

How many Bible Scriptures are you able to recite? I am sure there are many good brothers and sisters in Christ who are able to let many Bible verses roll off of their tongues, quote entire Psalms, know how many books are in the Bible and their proper order; but the purpose of this book is to discuss forms of witness that are easy to perform, as the book's subtitle is *99 Easy Ways to Witness*. So, with this fact in mind, we will strive to keep it simple and easy. You are aware that in order for you to become involved in a meaningful witness ministry you, as well as I, must learn and remember Bible Scriptures.

Although there are hundreds of Scriptures that we could list in this chapter, we have held the list to a total of twenty-one. You will notice that the Scriptures have been arranged in groups of seven. I challenge you to take the first group of seven Scriptures and learn them, so that before you retire to your bedroom tonight, you will be able to recite them. When you awaken the next morning, give yourself the test to assure that the first group of scriptures will become locked into your brain cells to recall whenever the opportunity arises to use them in your witness to others. You will notice that below each group of seven, there is a statement declaring that you have met the challenge to learn the Bible Scriptures, a place for you to sign your name and write in the date you learned them. Now, perhaps this is a bit more involved than flying a Christian flag, or placing a Bible on the dashboard of your automobile; but learning seven Scriptures is still a relatively easy task for you.

After learning verses in the first group, I challenge you to continue on—at your own pace—to learn the remaining verses. † When you learn this entire group of Scriptures, you will have added ammunition to be more powerful in the spirit of your witness.

1. *In everything you do, put God first and He will direct you and crown your efforts with success.* (Proverbs 3:6 TLB)

2. *Anyone who calls upon the name of the Lord will be saved.* (Romans 10:13 TLB)

3. *Come close to God and He will come close to you.* (James 4:8 NEB)

4. *Jesus said, "This is my commandment; love one another, as I have loved you. There is no greater love than this, that a man should lay down his life for his friends."* (John 15:12 NEB)

5. *Jesus said, "Let not your heart be troubled; ye believe in God, believe also in me. In my Father's house are many mansions; if it were not so I would have told you. I go to prepare a place for you."* (John 14:1-2 KJV)

6. *When Jesus spoke again to the people, He said, "I am the light of the world. Whoever follows me will never walk in darkness, but will have the light of life."* (John 8:12 NIV)

7. *Jesus said, "And lo, I am with you always even unto the end of the world."* (Matthew 28:20 KJV)

This is to declare that I have learned the above Scriptures and I will use them in my witness to others.

Signed_____ Date_____

8. *Jesus said, "Everything is possible for him that believes."* (Mark 9:23 NIV)

9. *And we know that all things work together for good to them that love God.* (Romans 9:28 KJV)

10. *Don't store up treasures here on earth where they can erode away or may be stolen. Store them in heaven where they will never lose their value and are safe from thieves.* (Matthew 6:19-20 TLB)

11. *No eye has seen, nor ear has heard, no mind has conceived what God has prepared for those who love him.* (1 Corinthians 2:9 NIV)

12. *Believe in the Lord Jesus Christ and thou shalt be saved.* (Acts 16:31 KJV)

13. *For God so loved the world that He gave His only begotten Son, that whosoever believeth in Him should not perish, but have everlasting life.* (John 3:16 KJV)

14. *Jesus answered, "And said unto him, verily, verily, I say unto thee, except a man be born again he cannot see the kingdom of God."* (John 3:3 KJV)

This is to declare that I have learned the above Scriptures, and I will use them in my witness to others.

Signed_____ Date_____

15. *The Lord is my shepherd, I shall not want .* (Psalm 23:1 RSV)

16. *Jesus said to him, "I am the way, and the truth, and the life; no one comes to the Father, but by me."* (John 14:6 RSV)

17. *Jesus Christ is the same yesterday and today and forever.* (Hebrews 13:8 NIV)

18. *For where two or three come together in my name (Jesus), there am I with them.* (Matthew 18:20 NIV)

20. *Do not love the world or anything in the world. If anyone loves the world, the love of the Father is not in him.* (1 John 2:15 NIV)

21. *Jesus said, "...For what shall it profit a man, if he shall gain the whole world, and lose his own soul? Or what shall a man give in exchange for his soul?"* (Mark 8:36-37 KJV)

This is to declare that I have learned the above Scriptures, and I will use them in my witness to others.

Signed_____ Date_____

Well, here they are—twenty-one easy-to-learn Bible Scriptures. I encourage you to learn them, and when these Scriptures have been learned, expand your Scriptural knowledge by learning more. We need to know the Scriptures, be able to quote them, and know where they are located. † In closing this chapter, the easy witness message is to learn to recite Bible verses.

CHAPTER 55
Tract 'em Down

One of the oldest ways that I remember folks witnessing is in the form of gospel tracts. You know the ones I am speaking about—you find them placed in public restrooms, telephone booths, and other places just waiting for someone to pick up and read. I have wondered, just who does pick up these printed gospel tracts? I often feel the urge to pick up one, but I leave it with the hopes that another person will pick it up and be led into the kingdom.

One of the fondest ways that I recall receiving a gospel tract happened three years ago. I love wild birds and feed them regularly. I provide many bird houses for bird nesting and housing. When the early spring arrives I wait anxiously for the Purple Martin birds, and other species, to arrive. While shopping at an open-air flea market I came to a stand where an elderly gentleman had a good supply of bird houses for sale. They were hand-crafted by this senior citizen and were a bit crudely constructed; however, they suited my purpose, and I really liked the price. He was offering them at five dollars for two bird houses. † When I arrived home and examined the houses closer, I discovered that the gentleman had placed a four page printed brochure into each bird house proclaiming a message of salvation. How about you, fellow Christians, do you make a craft item, manufacture a product, or sell something in which you could witness to your patrons by placing a gospel tract within or about your product in some way?

We all know that gospel tracts are available through many sources. There are many styles and formats. Of all that I have seen, I personally like the ones printed and made available by Chick Publications of California. They are printed in many different languages and are shipped around the world. Their tracts are neatly illustrated in cartoon form, which makes easy reading and keeps the reader's interest on the subject.

With the permission of the publishers, we are reprinting a portion of one of my favorite Chick Publications entitled *The Execution:*

Did you know that someone was executed for YOU? This person loves you more than anyone else ever could. God sent His Son, Jesus, to earth to be executed for you. Jesus shed His blood (God's blood) to wash away your sins, so you can go to heaven.

© 1992 by Jack T. Chick

A big selection of Chick tracts on various subjects is available at Christian book stores, or you may write Chick Publications direct. Their address is: Chick Publications, P.O. Box 662, Chino, California 91708-0662.

CHAPTER 56
Join Up

There are many well-planned, beneficial organizations that allow us to join forces with others and give us the opportunity to witness to our faith. One of my favorites is an organization based around those who are involved in Christian ministry that includes motorcyclists.

The group is organized under the name of Christian Motorcyclists Association. The CMA is not a Christian club or a riding group designed to segregate Christians from the influences of the world, but rather, it is a ministry designed to thrust its members into the mission of spreading the light of Jesus into the darkest areas. The group now claims 54,000 members, and their main purpose is to share the Gospel with motorcyclists. This is achieved by attending motorcycle events, offering their time and skills as servants, and conducting worship services. Their claim is that thousands have come to Christ as a result of these efforts.

Membership is open to non-motorcycle riders, also; and they would welcome your inquiry. One of CMA's mottos is: "Do you want to know the best way to chase the darkness? Be a light!" (Christian Motorcyclists Association, P.O. Box 9, Hatfield, AR 71945)

As stated earlier, there are many Christian organizations awaiting your interest and support. Suggestion: Check with your local churches, civic organizations, Chamber of Commerce, and, perhaps, your local newspaper. † There just may be a Christian organization of interest that you will want to join, serve and witness. Your light may shine a bit brighter when you join a Christian group!

CHAPTER 57
Pass it On

When the last page of this book is read, you will arrive at a point where a decision must be made. What will happen to this book? Will you place it on a book shelf with other books that have been gathered there for years and, perhaps, become a permanent part of your book collection; or will you place it on your desk to use as a reference book that will remind you to continue being a witnessing person?

How about this option? † Take the book with you to your workplace for others to see. It may capture the attention of a co-worker, compelling him to pick it up for a closer examination. Be on your toes—anyone who looks at the book will ask questions, and you will need to know the contents to be able to answer the resulting inquiries. So, if you choose this option, be sure to read the book prior to placing it on your workplace desk, counter, etc.

† Another way you may consider the future of this book is to simply decide to share it with others by passing it along to someone. † You may ask him to pass it on to another when he is finished reading it, or you may wish to have it returned to you. It's your choice; but please keep in mind, if this book is stored away, it will not be a witness to anyone. Won't you pass it on? Don't hide it!

"You are the world's light—a city on a hill, glowing in the night for all to see. Don't hide your light! Let it shine for all; let your good deeds flow for all to see, so that they will praise your heavenly Father." (Matthew 5:14-16 TLB)

CHAPTER 58
Stick 'em Up

For this easy witness project, I must ask you to jour-ney to your favorite Christian bookstore. Take a walk through, and when you come to the rack that contains stickers, stop to look over the selections. Buy a pack-age or two of your choosing. I recently purchased two packages at about one dollar each, and they each con-tained a couple of dozen stickers. The ad copy on the back of the package exclaimed, "Just peel and stick—ideal to decorate. Place on envelopes, notebooks, gifts, and almost anywhere." The individual stickers had these messages printed on them in brilliant colors:

- *Love one another.*
- *Love lifted me.*
- *Give your ♥ to Jesus.*
- *Love the Lord with all your ♥.*
- *Thank you, Jesus*
- *Smile—God loves you.*
- *God is love.*
- *Praise the Lord.*
- *I love Sunday School.*
- *Who makes the flowers grow?*

Okay, now I have the stickers. What can I do with them? † I first took the stickers to church, and dur-ing the visitation time, I wandered around the congre-gation, seeking out the little people, and planted a sticker on their clothing. They seemed pleased to re-ceive the stickers as most kids do like them.

Then I began to devise other ways I could witness with stickers. † I thought about my briefcase that I use almost daily and placed on it a red heart that con-tained the message, "Love lifted me." I see it each day, and it is almost like witnessing to myself.

At this point, one could let his imagination run with

the idea and dream up many ways to witness with stickers such as placing them on telephone receivers, bumpers, windows, trash containers, lawn mowers, bird houses, bicycles, motorcycles, luggage, notebooks, and other personal items. Just stick 'em on, and let them be a witness for you and others to see!

CHAPTER 59
Pizza and Prayer

Just when I thought I had come to the end of my list of easy ways to witness Jesus in my life, my daughter, Doneen, came home from an evening of fun and fellowship with her church's youth group organization. † She stated that her group had gone to our local Pizza Hut restaurant for fellowship and an evening meal.

The rain clouds rolled in, and that stormy night became a great time to enjoy a leisurely meal. The youth leader, Kathryn Self, proclaimed that after the meal she gave each young person a new Bible, and they began to hold a prayer and Bible study right there in those busy surroundings. Yes, it was busy, and it was a noisy environment, she related, but they continued to do what she called God's will right there. I wonder how many customers were in that busy restaurant that rainy evening. The management and food servers were excellent hosts and welcomed the youth group back anytime they wished to meet and eat.

CHAPTER 60
Easy Ways Others Witness

This chapter is a lengthy one that tells others' witnessing ways. Some are famous individuals that you will probably recognize, and some are not so famous. However, the important part is that all these people are being featured because of their Christian witness.

Sing Out The Witness!
Doyle Lawson is well known among the many fans who follow the fast-growing music known as Bluegrass. Bluegrass music festivals and shows are promoted throughout the United States and are even capturing audiences in many foreign countries including Japan. This music has the reputation of being fast-paced entertainment, and the entertainers involved in this music are dedicated to keeping the shows clean and pleasing to all those in attendance. Doyle Lawson's group travels the country billed as Doyle Lawson & Quicksilver. † My reason for including him in this chapter is to commend him for taking the time—while on stage entertaining—to give praise and thanks to his Lord and Master. He lets his light shine each time he goes before an audience.

Another long time Country-Bluegrass entertainer who professed his faith to his many fans through the years was a top-notch, lovable country fiddler who was known as Chubby Wise. † During the last years he was on earth, he never performed anywhere that he did not stop for a few moments to thank God and praise Him for the many blessings sent his way.

While on the subject of music entertainers, one that is currently a show headliner and Grand Ole Opry regular is Ricky Skaggs. † Ricky, along with his entertaining wife, Sharon White (of the family singing group,

The Whites), let their lights shine brightly to project a Christian image wherever they entertain. Of course, I am only mentioning a few of the many fine Christians in the field of music who profess their faith on radio, TV, and stage performances.

Singers, you have a captive audience when you are performing; won't you consider sharing Jesus' love with them? It will only take a moment; fellow Christians will know where you stand, and it will be very much appreciated.

Teachers Cannot Witness in Public Schools, Can They?

Picture this! You are a teacher in a public high school. You are in contact with students five days per week. As a Christian, you feel the urge to witness to the young people that you teach, but to do so places you in violation of school policies and procedures. In fact, there are federal laws that prohibit teachers from spouting out their religious beliefs to their students.

Please keep in mind the quoted statement from our first president, George Washington. He said, "It is impossible to rightly govern the world without God or the Bible." When our founding fathers signed their names to the Declaration of Independence, they believed that God was the only sure foundation upon which to build a nation that would endure. These men knew that this unique experiment in freedom would only stand the test of time by God's grace. Something is wrong with America when teachers need to keep mum on religious matters while our children are under their supervision.

When I once spoke with a teacher friend of mine, he related to me his ways of revealing his faith in God to the many students who are in his classes. I was startled by his statement because I had heard other teachers say they leave their religion off the school grounds, and while in class, do not ever show any signs of having religious convictions. My friend revealed that he, first of all, lives his life so that it will reflect a life of high moral quality. This will assure others he does have spiritual convictions. In speaking his faith, he polls his students on various subjects during the school year. He will ask the group, "How many attend worship service regularly?" In years past, he has noted that the percentage was sixty percent or more. However, his most recent poll revealed that the percentage of his students who attend church regularly is a shockingly low twenty percent.

While discussing the students' church attendance, the question has come from a student, "Say, teacher, what about yourself? Do you attend church?" When a question is asked by a student to a teacher, he is obligated to answer in some detail, although he must do so with some tact. He can relate where he attends church, how long he has been a member, details about the youth program, and other things he wants to say to answer the student's question.

Another way this teacher reveals his faith is when students become disgusted with themselves because of a bad test result or failure to perform a sports-related activity. He may take the time to pause and tell the student, † "Don't worry; we still love you!" My friend went on to explain, "By now, most of my students are aware that I am a God-fearing, spiritual man, and they are not really too surprised when I answer, 'we,' meaning the Lord and I."

In my interview with my teacher friend, I was also intrigued with his church bulletin witness story. † After the bulletin has served its purpose for the Sunday worship service, he takes it to his high school. When he performs his teaching duties each week, it's tucked away in a coat pocket waiting for an opportune time to retrieve it. He says it usually works something like this, "In searching for something on which to write a note or take down a phone number, I will take out the bulletin and exclaim, 'It's my church bulletin from Sunday. It comes in handy sometimes.' It lets folks around me in the school system know that I went to church that previous Sunday. Or, how about this one," he continues, "We are all gathered in the lunch room and I spot a student way across the room who often attends the youth gathering at my church. In a voice that is a bit louder than usual, I yell out, † 'Don't forget the youth program at church tonight!'"

Before ending the interview, I bluntly asked my teacher friend, "Are you not concerned that someone along the way might reprimand you for your witness, even though it is somewhat subdued?" "It has worked for me a long time. I love my students and they know I care for them—their physical being as well as their souls. I've always felt that God will look over me, guide me, and bless me for my stand with my students."

Donna Douglas

We all remember Donna Douglas as the very beautiful and talented actress who portrayed "Elly May Clampett" in the long running television production *The Beverly Hillbillies* (1962-1971). Today Miss Douglas is involved in religious activities, speaking and witnessing to her faith in churches and other places that want her to speak.

I have met Donna on several occasions where she was invited to be a guest celebrity at film festivals which my family and I have attended. She has proven herself to be a really nice person who loves people and blends in nicely with her bubbling personality and her ability to make folks very comfortable around her.

Of course, almost everyone at the film festivals wanted to get a picture taken with Donna and take home an autographed photograph. She has a divine way of witnessing. When she autographs she takes a marking type pen and writes in large letters and numbers. † Here is the way she autographed a photo to my daughter Doneen. *Doneen, You're special, Donna Douglas (Elly May).* Underneath her signature, she includes *Proverbs 3:5-6 (If you want favor with both God and man, and a reputation for good judgment and common sense, then trust the Lord completely; don't ever trust yourself. In everything you do, put God first, and He will direct you and crown your efforts with success (TLB)).* I think this is a very special way that she lets her light shine for Jesus.

The Family Circus

Bil Keene is the cartoonist who illustrates the popular comic strip *The Family Circus.* The strip is carried daily by newspapers coast to coast. † Mr. Keene constantly lets his light shine by illustrating religious themes in his strip. Recently, two newspaper cartoons appeared that caught my attention. One showed a small boy praying and the caption read "... and last, but not least, Dear Lord, take care of yourself. If you don't we're all in trouble." A few weeks later, he illustrated a small girl coming out of church speaking to her father saying, "Our Sunday school teacher must be Jesus' grandmother 'cause she talks about him all the time." Mr. Keene is to be commended for taking the time to incorporate his religious input into the comic strip page in the many newspapers in which his strip appears.

Barbers Can Witness Too!

A Christian gentleman in our small town owns and operates two businesses in the same building. He is both a locksmith and a barber. If you are locked out, locked in, need keys made, or want to have your hair trimmed—Mr. Leroy Taylor is the one you need to see. His barber shop may be similar to the one on the popular television show that involves another man named "Taylor" who happens to be the sheriff in the fictitious town of Mayberry on *The Andy Griffith Show.* Mr. Taylor's barber shop, like Floyd's Barber Shop, also boasts of having two barber chairs.

† While sitting around the shop getting a haircut or just catching up on the local news, the television in the corner is tuned to a station that programs Chris-

tian Gospel music featuring favorite Gospel singers. Each time I visit the shop I always think: Leroy is witnessing to his faith by programming Gospel music throughout the day. When questioned if he ever thought of the television in the corner being a form of a witness, he shrugged a bit and stated, "I play what I like to hear hoping others will like it too. Sometimes I get a better message from a song than from a preacher."

Thank You, Customers

A business owner in our area has a practice of writing a detailed thank-you letter at the end of each month to all customers who make a purchase from their sales location during that month. In the letter he personally thanks them for the trust they have placed in the company and expresses his appreciation for their business. † The owner also informs the customers that the company from which they have made their purchase is Christian owned and operated, and that the purchaser's satisfaction is of utmost importance to the business. Others who may decide to purchase from the company may be assured that honesty and fair dealings are high on the owner's priority list. The thank-you letters are signed off, "May God Bless You!"

Show Me The Money

For many years, Irene Nelson has been involved in a witness project that has been of interest to others as well as myself. She purchases replica prints of what appears to be a United States five dollar bill on one side, and when you turn it over, there is a message relating to what money can and cannot buy. The money message includes that what money cannot buy, Jesus Christ will give freely without charge.

† Irene inserts one of the replica $5.00 printed bills in each letter or card she mails. When asked why she used this method to witness she replied, "I just want to help spread the word of salvation."

Auto Dealership

✝ Recently, I read a story about the owner of a large automobile dealership who places a Bible in the glove compartment of each new and used vehicle purchased. Now this is a powerful witness on the part of that business owner. The businessman is telling his customers that he is a Christian. Conducting his business in a Christian manner, he truly appreciates his customers and wishes to share Jesus with others. Perhaps other auto agency officials will read this witness and make Bible-placing a part of their sales plan.

Van der Noots

The Jacquire Van der Noots family of Apopka, Florida, wrote our publishing company recently, and our eyes quickly focused on a quiet, easy Christian witness that appeared on the envelope containing their order. ✝ Their name and address were printed on one of those peel and stick return address labels. After the last line of their address was the statement, "Christ is the answer."

Jim & John

Brothers Jim and John Moss of Huntsville, Alabama, share their Christianity in a number of ways. ✝ They make copies of selected materials and pass them out to friends and co-workers. ✝ They also purchased 200 copies of Harold Morris' book *Twice Pardoned* and gave them out to selected persons. The Moss brothers sent a copy to me; I read it with interest, and afterwards, mailed it along to an inmate friend at the county jail. From the moment I first shared with them my plans for writing this book, they have been very supportive and interested in seeing its completion. Both plan to include it as one of the ways they witness to others. Jim and John are big boosters of the Cross In My Pocket Ministry, always giving away those little shining crosses. ✝ The closing in a recent letter I received from John struck me as another easy way to witness. It read, "In Christ, our only hope, John Moss."

Connie Hopper

My friend, Connie, who is a member of the Southern Gospel singing group, The Hoppers, not only witnesses as she travels and sings with the group, but she praises God in another very important way. † Connie is a cancer survivor, and has written a book about this experience titled, *The Peace that Passeth Understanding.* She begins her book by quoting Philippians 4:7 KJV: *The peace of God, which passeth all understanding, shall keep your hearts and minds through Jesus Christ.* Throughout this bout with cancer, Connie prayed, "Lord, whatever it takes to bring my life to what You would have it, let it be." Connie reminded us that we learn through our sufferings, and thanks God for hers. Numerous people have read this comforting book and have been blessed by it.

Chick-Fil-A

Chick-Fil-A restaurants are located from coast-to-coast and are known for their tasty food, especially their special way of preparing chicken. Their food serving stores are found mostly in malls and shopping areas throughout the United States. † It is the store policy not to open on Sunday anytime at any location. It is my understanding that most shopping malls require tenants to be open when the malls are open, but not Chick-Fil-A. Somehow, they are exempt from that regulation of opening on Sunday.

While on the subject of operating a business on Sunday, I would not be the one to tell any business owner whether to open their business doors on Sunday; that is solely the decision of the individual business owner. However, I know that it would be wrong for me to allow my business to open on Sundays. I suppose that the corporate heads of Chick-Fil-A have made the decision, as I have, not to open their business on Sundays.

Without judging others, I would just say that through my eyes, the Chick-Fil-A corporation is surely letting their light shine in their special way. Recently, I witnessed a newly installed sign at several of their shopping mall locations. The sign reads:

> *Our Corporate Purpose*
> † *To glorify God by being a faithful stew-ard of all that He has entrusted to us and to have a positive influence on all those who come in contact with Chick-Fil-A.*

Surely, the presence of our Lord is felt throughout the Chick-Fil-A organization.

Thrifty Witness

Thrifty Nickel is the name of a weekly classified ad newspaper that reaches 90,000 readers in the central part of North Carolina. If you want to buy a sewing machine, a shotgun, or even an automobile, you can probably find it in this neatly printed tabloid newspaper.

Each Thursday, when I pick up my copy, I always look at the top of the front page to see which Bible verse appears there. A recent issue displayed in bold print for 90,000 readers to see, *Our help is in the name of the Lord, who made Heaven and Earth.* (Psalm 1:24)

† This publishing house is letting its light shine by making space available every week for a Bible verse. It doesn't take much space, and it undoubtedly causes numerous readers to think about God when they see it.

In all likelihood, there is a *Thrifty Nickel* or similar-type newspaper being published and distributed in your hometown. Do they offer their readers space where God's word is proclaimed? If your answer is no, my next question is, would you like to see news-print space provided for that purpose? † Write or phone the marketplace newspaper, inform them of the

Thrifty Nickel witness and ask them to consider allotting space each week. You may even offer to contribute the Bible verses each week. Your contribution just may be their deciding factor to comply with your suggestion.

Branson, Missouri—God's Special Place

Anita Bryant is known by most who have lived on this planet for the past thirty-plus years. Miss Bryant was runner-up in the Miss America Contest in 1958 while representing her home state of Oklahoma. She has been a mainstay throughout the world with her television, radio, and singing career. She went along with Bob Hope and his troupe of entertainers eight times around the globe to entertain our armed forces gals and guys at Christmas time.

While vacationing in Branson, Missouri, my family and I discovered that Anita and her husband Charlie had purchased a theater there and that Anita was presenting her singing variety show nightly except for Sundays. † Each Sunday morning, she has an all-Gospel music program that includes her personal testimony and greatly inspires God's people. My family attended and was spiritually moved by being in the presence of this woman of God. I know of no one who I believe is stronger in the faith than Anita Bryant. After being in her presence for that Sunday morning gathering, I believe that (as *Webster's Dictionary* defines prophet) Anita is "a person inspired by God to speak for Him."

† In spite of her busy schedule, Anita takes the time to conduct a group Bible study each Friday at her theater for her band members, theater staff, and other Branson entertainers who care to be a part of this Bible study. Her daily life is much of her witness.

The Branson, Missouri, area is a very special place where God's people can be entertained by those who appreciate good family values. We have attended more than thirty different shows during the four times we have visited, and not once have we heard a joke or remark on stage that was in bad taste. We've heard no profanity, no racial slurs, or anything of that nature. It is obvious to us that Branson, Missouri, is a very special place on this earth where families can see quality entertainment from headliners including: Andy Williams, Tony Orlando, Mel Tillis, Charlie Pride, The Oak Ridge Boys, Anita Bryant, Bobby Vinton, The Osmond Brothers, Roy Clark, Mickey Gilley, Barbara Fairchild, and a host of others. Many of the entertainers there build their faith in God into their personal and professional lives.

The Braschler Family stands out strongly in their faith. The Braschlers proudly † display the Christian flag as a permanent fixture on the stage where three daily shows are performed. What a witness! Think about that. How many times have you seen a Christian flag on a stage of any kind outside of a church? † Also, as you first enter this beautiful theater, you will notice that on the wall of the lobby is a large painting of an angel with trumpet in hand; at the other end, an angel is playing a harp. To top off this witness are the printed words in large bold letters, **THE KING IS COMING.**

The preceding has been a brief sketch of some special human beings who live and serve the Lord in Branson, Missouri. If good, clean, wholesome entertainment is of interest to you in a place where God and the flag are still respected—Branson is the place we recommend. My family and I are planning another trip there very soon. The town people, the entertainment, and the Ozark Mountains with all of their glory— on a scale of one to ten we give Branson, Missouri, a ten plus.

Lord, Let Us Thank You

Kathy and Tommy Hildreth witness when they patronize eating establishments. † Prior to the partaking of their meals, they pause to thank God for the food they are about to receive. This effort, they believe, is a witness to other restaurant diners when they take time to pray in a public place.

Jimmy & Rosalyn Carter

A noteworthy and most outstanding Christian witness is former President, Jimmy Carter. During his Presidency, he never hid his born-again Christian faith. He has spent much of his lifetime trying to live his Christian faith. Teaching Sunday School has been part of his life since he was eighteen years old. Carter says when someone who hasn't known Christ or had a relationship with God tells him they have accepted Christ because of something he said or wrote, that gives him a great sense of accomplishment. Carter has been giving Bible lessons at his church (Maranatha) almost from the time he left the White House. There are only about thirty families in the church; however, there are usually at least 200 people from all faiths present for his classes each Sunday.

Both former President Carter and his wife, Rosalyn, are very active in Habitat for Humanity. They go out and help build houses for the poor, just the same as the other volunteers—hammering nails, etc. right alongside everyone else.

Mr. Carter's latest book, *Sources of Strength*, is a collection of Sunday School lessons that he has taught through the years and is available at bookstores. I am proud to have it in our home library, and I am glad that this Christian twosome had the opportunity to witness to the entire world by serving our country as the President and First Lady.

No Ordinary Bookmark

Billy Mills, an insurance agent, has a way of witnessing that I was not aware of. When we purchased a life insurance policy for our daughter, Doneen, Billy presented us with a bookmark. It was no ordinary bookmark, as it was made of silk, and on it were instructions regarding how to use the Bible. Through the years, I have found it to be quite useful in locating special items of interest. Perhaps you also will find it to be helpful in your study of the Bible.

How to Use the Bible

When in sorrow
    Read John 14
When men fail you
    Read Psalm 27
When you have sinned
    Read Psalm 51
When you worry
    Read Matthew 6:19-34
When you are in danger
    Read Psalm 91
If you have the blues
    Read Psalm 34
When God seems far away
    Read Psalm 139
If you are discouraged
    Read Isaiah 40
If you are lonely or fearful
    Read Psalm 23
If you feel down and out
    Read Romans 8:39
When you want courage for your task
    Read Joshua 1
When the world seems bigger than God
    Read Psalm 90
When you want rest and peace
    Read Matthew 11:25-30
When leaving home for labor or travel
    Read Psalm 121: 107:23-31
If you get bitter or critical
    Read 1st Corinthians 13
If thinking of investments and returns
    Read Mark 10:17-31
For a great invitation—A great opportunity
    Read Isaiah 55

God Loves You
BILLY L. MILLS

Church on Sunday

Everywhere I go I see the Gospel of Jesus Christ uplifted. Witness messages do not always jump out at you—many times you have to look around, behind, up, and down to see them. Recently, while visiting Surfside Beach, South Carolina, Noreen brought to my attention a very simple witness at a business location. On the front entrance door was a mounted sign that revealed the hours that the bookstore was open for business. Below is a reproduction of the sign.

```
THE BOOK RACK
Surfside Beach, SC
       Hours
Mon. ............. 10-5
Tues. ........... 10-5
Wed. ............ 10-5
Thurs. .......... 10-5
Fri. ................ 10-5
Sat. .............. 10-5
CHURCH ON SUNDAY
```

Jesus Loves You

Dianne Campbell of Morganton, North Carolina, uses her telephone to witness to everyone who dials her number. She personally answers her ringing telephone by greeting her callers with the message, "Jesus loves you."

We are interested in acquiring more ways that you and others witness to your faith. Write the publisher: Empire Publishing, Inc., PO Box 717, Madison, NC 27025. If your contributions are selected, they will appear in a reprinted version of *Let Your Light Shine.*

About the Author

Don was born in Mount Airy, North Carolina, and lived there for the first nine years of his life prior to moving to Madison, North Carolina, where he lives today.

After graduating from high school, Don joined the United States Navy. During his three-year enlistment, he was stationed at various naval air stations. For the last year of his tour of duty, he was assigned to the aircraft carrier U.S.S. Ranger.

A short while after completing his military commitment, he married Noreen Cox in 1959; they will soon celebrate forty years of marriage. Don and Noreen have two wonderful daughters, Rhonda and Doneen, a caring son-in-law, Stephen, and an adorable grandson, Nathan.

Because of his love for vintage movies, in 1974, Don founded Empire Publishing Company and began publishing *The Big Reel*, a monthly publication for movie fans and collectors worldwide. After twenty years of publishing *The Big Reel*, it was sold to another company, and Empire began to concentrate on book publishing. Over the years, the publishing company has originated and distributed more than twenty secular books including *The Roy Rogers Book*, *The Gene Autry Book*, *Randolph Scott/ A Film Biography*, and *Blue Moon of Kentucky*, a bluegrass music book, among others. *Let Your Light Shine* is the first (but hopefully not the last) Christian book published by Empire Publishing.

Brother Don

Afterword

In over twenty years of ministry, I have constantly seen a real need among many Christians for help and instruction concerning how to effectively witness to and share the Faith. This book contains the clearest and simplest methods I have seen for sharing Christian witness. Why no one has ever come up with such a book before now, I do not know! But I do know that by using at least some of the methods discussed in this book, you can begin to share your faith in new and exciting ways. We need both grace and knowledge to be good witnesses for Christ (II Peter 3:18). God will provide the grace, but we must do our part to gain the knowledge. We have the answer for which all men are searching, and His name is Jesus Christ. And yet His message of forgiveness and redeeming love is a well-kept secret among many Christians. Therefore, let us begin to share our faith in Him—in simple ways at first, and then in more bold and direct ways as the Lord leads and as we grow—but let us begin!

Finally, please do not place this volume on a bookshelf or in a drawer to be soon forgotten, but pass it on for someone else to use. But most important of all, do all that you can—using what you have learned herein—to share your faith and to help others to *Behold the Lamb of God, which taketh away the sin of the world.* (John 1:29 KJV)   May God bless you as you do so!

Steve D. Joyce
Pastor

Other Books Available from Empire Publishing:

Alan Jackson: Gone Country by Mark Bego
Allan "Rocky" Lane, Republic's Action Ace by David Rothel
Andy Griffith Show, The, by Richard Kelly
Barbara Streisand Scrapbook, The, by Waldman
Black Hollywood by Gary Null
Blue Moon of Kentucky: Country and Bluegrass Music by Les Leverett
Bluegrass Music Cookbook by John F. Blair
Bluegrass: A History by Neil V. Rosenberg
Bob Wills: Hubbin' It by Ruth Sheldon
Brady Bunch Book, The, by Andrew J. Edelstein and Frank Lovece
Branson, Missouri Scrapbook, The, by Scott Faragher
Charlie Chan and the Movies by Ken Hanke
"Cheers" Trivia Book, The, by Mark Wenger
Classic TV Westerns by Ronald Jackson
Classics of the Horror Film by William K. Everson
Classics of the Gangster Film by Robert Bookbinder
Complete Films of Buster Keaton by Jim Kline
Complete Films of Cary Grant by Donald Deschner
Complete Films of Humphrey Bogart by Clifford McCarthy
Complete Films of McDonald and Eddy by Philip Castanza
Complete Films of Laurel and Hardy by William K. Everson
Dave's World: Guide to the Late Show with David Letterman
Dick Powell Story, The, by Tony Thomas
Don't Look Up! Virginia UFO Sightings by Gordon and Dellinger
Essential Hank Williams, The, by Tim Jones
Film Encyclopedia, The
Films and Career of Audie Murphy, The, by Sue Gossett
Films of Betty Grable, The, by Ed Hulse
Films of Clint Eastwood by Boris Zmijewsky and Lee Pfeiffer
Films of Dustin Hoffman by Douglas Brode
Films of Frank Sinatra by Gene Ringgold and Clifford McCarty
Films of Hopalong Cassidy, The, by Francis M. Nevins, Jr.
Films of Johnny Mack Brown, The, by John A. Rutherford
Films of Sean Connery by Lee Pfeiffer and Philip Lisa
Films of Shirley Temple by Robert Windeler
Films of Tom Hanks by Lee Pfeiffer and Michael Lewis
Final Curtain: Deaths of Noted Movie & TV Personalities
Gene Autry Reference - Trivia - Scrapbook, The, by David Rothel
George Jones: I Lived to Tell It All with Tom Carter
Gone with the Wind: The Complete Trivia Book by Pauline Bartel
Great Baseball Films by Rob Edelman
Growing Up Brady: I Was a Teenage Greg by Barry Williams

Hank Snow Story, The, by Hank Snow
Hank Williams: From Life to Legend by Jerry Rivers
Hollywood Musical, The, by Tony Thomas
I Fall to Pieces: The Music and Life of Patsy Cline by Mark Bego
I Love Lucy: The Complete Picture History by Michael McClay
I Was that Masked Man by Clayton Moore
In Close Harmony: The Story of the Louvin Brothers by Charles Wolfe
Jimmie Rodgers: America's Blue Yodeler by Nolan Porterfield
Lash LaRue: The Man, Not the Legend by Charles M. Sharpe
Life and Films of Buck Jones, The, by Buck Rainey
Life Everlaughter by Jerry Clower
Little Rascals by Leonard Maltin and Richard Bann
Lon Chaney: The Man Behind the Thousand Faces by Michael Blake
Moe Howard and the Three Stooges by Moe Howard
More Character People by McClure, Twomey and Jones
More Cowboy Shooting Stars by Rutherford and Smith
901 Best Jokes There Ever Was, The, by J. R. Miller
Official Andy Griffith Show Scrapbook by Lee Pfeiffer
Official Dick Van Dyke Show, The, by Vince Waldron
Partridge Family Album by Joey Green
Randolph Scott / A Film Biography by Jefferson Brim Crow, III
Round-Up, The, by Donald R. Key
Real Bob Steele and a Man Called Brad, The, by Bob Nareau
Republic Chapterplays, The, by R. M. Hayes
Roy Rogers Reference - Trivia - Scrapbook, The, by David Rothel
Saddle Gals by Edgar M. Wyatt and Stever Turner
Saddle Pals by Garv Towell and Wayne E. Keates
Satisfied Mind, A: The Country Music Life of Porter Wagoner by Eng
Stars of Country Music, edited by Bill C. Malone and Judith McCulloh
Stroke of Fortune by Willim C. Cline
The Best of Universal by Tony Thomas
Three Stooges Scrapbook by Jeff Lenburg
Tim Holt by David Rothel
Tom Mix Highlights by Andy Woytowich
Trail Talk by Bobby J. Copeland
Travolta by Dave Thompson
Universal Horrors by Michael Brunas, John Brunas, and Tom Weaver
Whatever Happened to Randolph Scott? by C. H. Scott

According to the book of St. Mark, in the New Testament, one of the last things Jesus said before returning to his heavenly home was:

. . . Go ye into all the world and preach the gospel to every creature. (St. Mark 16:15 KJV)